Discovering and Developing Talent in Schools

Also available:

Curriculum Provision for the Gifted and Talented in the Primary School – Edited by Deborah Eyre and Lynne McClure (1 85346 771 5)

Curriculum Provision for the Gifted and Talented in the Secondary School – Edited by Deborah Eyre and Hilary Lowe (1 85346 772 3)

Teaching the Very Able Child: Developing a policy and adopting strategies for provision – Belle Wallace (1 85346 705 7)

Gifted and Talented Children with Special Educational Needs – Diane Montgomery (1 85346 831 2)

Gifted and Talented Learners: Creating a Policy for Inclusion – Barry Hymer and Deborah Michel (1 85346 955 6)

Thinking Skills and Problem-Solving: An Inclusive Approach – Belle Wallace *et al.* (1 84312 107 7)

Discovering and Developing Talent in Schools

An Inclusive Approach

Bette Gray-Fow

 David Fulton Publishers

National Association
for Able Children
in Education

To Ralph V. James, Director of my Junior High School Band.
His inclusive approach to discovering and developing talent made
all the difference.

David Fulton Publishers Ltd
The Chiswick Centre, 414 Chiswick High Road, London W4 5TF

www.fultonpublishers.co.uk

First published in Great Britain in 2005 by David Fulton Publishers

10 9 8 7 6 5 4 3 2 1

David Fulton Publishers is a division of Granada Learning Limited, part of ITV plc.

Note: The right of Bette Gray-Fow to be identified as the author of this work has been asserted by her in accordance with the Copyright, Designs and Patents Act 1988.

British Library Cataloguing in Publication Data
A catalogue record for this book is available from the British Library.

ISBN 1 84312 669 9

Typeset by FiSH Books, London
Printed and bound in Great Britain by Ashford Colour Press

Contents

NACE National Office
PO Box 242
Arnolds Way
Oxford OX2 9FR
Tel: 01865 861879
Fax: 01865 861880

**National Association
for Able Children
in Education**

NACE exists solely to support the daily work of teachers providing for pupils with high ability, whilst enabling all pupils to flourish.

We are a large association of professionals. We deliver advice, training and materials on learning and teaching, leadership and management, and whole-school improvement.

We provide:

- specialist advice and information to teachers, LEAs and government agencies
- courses – some in partnership with Granada Learning Professional Development and with optional online continuing support and access to tutors
- bespoke courses and guidance delivered at your premises
- tutors to work alongside teachers in the classroom
- annual and regional conferences
- market-leading books and seminal publications
- keynote speakers for special events
- support for special projects
- national and international links

Some of our most popular courses are linked to our best-selling books and delivered by the authors. These are opportunities to really understand new strategies and how to put them into practice.

Join us – membership gives you:

- quick access to professional advice and resources
- members' website for updates and exchange of practice
- termly newsletters, with practical articles and updates
- biannual journals with more substantial articles relating research to practical strategies
- discount on courses and conferences
- access to network of members and regional groups

Visit www.nace.co.uk for lists of publications, courses, services and to join NACE.

Advancing teaching: Inspiring able learners every day

Founded in 1984   Registered Charity No. 327230

Acknowledgements

There are many sources for the ideas and practical suggestions contained in this book. The first was growing up in my native Wisconsin, where – thanks to the opportunities offered at our local (state) schools – myself, my brother and my sister have all turned out to be either keen amateur or professional musicians. Another source has been all the valuable lessons learned (mostly by trial and error!) in working with young people in my role as a music teacher, both in schools and as a private instrumental/vocal teacher. (In fact, some of the experience goes back to my first teaching post here in the UK – now nearly 30 years ago.) A recent spell back in the classroom merely confirmed what I have always found: that the old adage 'There's talent on every street corner…what matters is what you *do* with it!' is absolutely true; that there really is talent in abundance, and that the key to developing it is hard work. I hope this book will go some way towards convincing you of this point of view.

As with most books, there is a long list of people to thank. First and foremost are the pupils and staff of the various schools where I have worked. They have contributed much to the thinking behind this book, and provided the direct stimulus for many of the practical suggestions for implementing an inclusive approach to finding and fostering talent in schools. Peter Desmond and Paul Harris provided encouragement and enthusiasm for the book, especially in the early stages. Professor Deborah Eyre first introduced me to this field; and her book *Able Children in Ordinary Schools* served as a constant source of inspiration. On a practical level, I would also like to thank: the Open University for granting me study leave in the spring of 2003, to work on the book; the House and Community of Launde Abbey, Leicestershire, which on several occasions provided a quiet place to write (and an interesting selection of fellow-guests, some of whose stories appear in this book!); Sophie Cox, whose formatting expertise gave the project a much-needed boost in its later stages; NACE, for useful comments on the content as the book developed. And last, but most emphatically not least, special thanks are owing to Margaret Marriott, my long-suffering editor at Fulton's. Her patience, encouragement and commitment to the project have been fundamental in seeing it through to its conclusion.

Any errors, omissions and confusions are, of course, my own.

I gratefully acknowledge the Qualifications and Curriculum Authority for permission to reproduce the National Curriculum guidelines for identifying talented pupils, in Appendix B.

About the author

Bette Gray-Fow is a freelance teacher, writer, consultant, trainer and musician. Formerly Creative Arts Team Leader/Lecturer in Education at the Open University and Senior Lecturer in the Research Centre for Able Pupils at Oxford Brookes University, she is also the author of *Chorus for Everyone* (Lindsay Music). As a researcher, she has investigated music technology provision nationally, leading the team which evaluated Youth Music's *Plug into Music Programme*, and authoring the report for publication on the web. As Director of Music in several schools, her departments were noted for the high quality of the singing, both in the classroom and in extracurricular groups; for the use of ICT, particularly for composition work; and for a range of independent learning strategies. Still active as a bassoonist, singer, choir trainer and teacher, she also adjudicates regularly for the British and International Federation of Festivals, and delivers workshops nationally on topics ranging from vocal technique for non-specialist music teachers to 'Finding – and fostering – the talent in everyone'. She can be contacted at bgf@discoveringtalent.com

Introduction

New developments stimulate new ways of looking at old issues. Here in the United Kingdom in the late 1990s the Department for Education and Employment (DfEE) – the major UK governmental body responsible for all aspects of education, and headed by the Secretary of State for Education – set out the following distinction between giftedness and talent, later elaborated in its *Excellence in Cities* (*EiC*) initiative (Ofsted 2001a, para. 26, p. 11):

■ *Giftedness* = either high attainment or potential/latent high ability in one or more 'academic' subjects.

■ *Talent* = either demonstrated attainment or latent ability in 'non-academic' areas, i.e. in the performing and visual arts, and in sport.[1]

This division runs counter to many previous models of giftedness and talent. Yet it is a distinction that relates well to people's conceptions of the realms in which talent operates. Think of 'talent-spotting' for potential in sport, 'talent shows' such as *Pop Idol* and *Fame Academy*, and a wealth of other uses for the term 'talented', many – but not all – of which relate to the arts and sport.

This book takes a fresh look at the whole issue of the so-called 'talent realm' (in DfES/*EiC* terms), and by re-examining many of our preconceptions about the nature and extent of talent

■ offers for discussion a model of giftedness and talent, based on the *EiC* distinction between 'academic' giftedness and 'non-academic' talent;

■ from this model argues for a new, more inclusive approach to 'talent spotting' in our schools and in the wider community – one which takes account of the unique nature of the talent realm;

■ hopes to increase awareness of the special needs of talented pupils, particularly as they impact on their primary and secondary school experiences.

---

1 Some authors have argued against this distinction between academic and artistic giftedness, e.g. Ellen Winner and Gail Martino, 'Giftedness in non-academic domains: the case of the visual arts and music', in K. A. Heller *et al.* (eds), *International Handbook of Giftedness and Talent* (2nd edition), Oxford: Elsevier Science Ltd, 2000, pp. 95–110.

The focus of Chapters 1 to 7 is on *discovering* talent. As well as dealing with some of the academic discussions surrounding the question 'what is talent?', they look at the overall benefits of the talent area for pupils (including early developers, late developers and all-rounders) and set out some practical strategies for identifying talented pupils.

Chapters 8, 9 and 10 look at *developing* talent, addressing the wider issue of what talented pupils are like, what they need, and what schools can realistically provide, both within and outside the curriculum.

The concluding chapter (Chapter 11) discusses some of the implications of using an inclusive approach to identify and foster talent.

In addition, there are four appendices at the back of the book: Appendix A provides an outline for a whole-school audit of provision for talented pupils; Appendix B contains the current National Curriculum guidelines for identifying talented pupils in PE, music, and art and design; Appendix C describes a Sheffield-based project designed to identify musically talented primary school pupils; and Appendix D provides guidance on writing whole-school and departmental policies for talent identification and development, and includes some sample policies.

What is talent?

Definition – a will-o'-the-wisp?

Anyone interested in gifted and talented education is aware that it involves an elusive concept, or set of concepts. We really don't know precisely what 'giftedness' is. We construct checklists based on the National Curriculum subject guidelines, or on the work of authors in the field, such as David George, Deborah Eyre, Joan Freeman, Belle Wallace and Barry Hymer. We analyse the behaviour of pupils we know (or even just suspect) of harbouring unusual gifts, and test them in a variety of ways. We undertake research into the way the brain works, using sophisticated scientific techniques. And always with the proviso that we don't know for sure if we're right.

Those who function as Gifted and Talented Coordinators in our primary and secondary schools have the added burden of trying to assemble lists of specific pupils, based on a variety of approaches.

While methods of identifying and providing for academically gifted pupils seem to be improving, the talent realm is proving to be more problematic.

In May 2003 the Office for Standards in Education (Ofsted), reporting on the impact of the *Excellence in Cities* initiative to raise achievement in inner-city schools, commented that:

> The focus on talented pupils is less well-developed in most schools.
>
> (Ofsted 2003, p. 4)

In particular, the inspectors felt that primary schools were 'far less adept at identifying talented pupils' than in identifying traditional concept academically able pupils; that 'few talented pupils in primary schools were taught by specialist teachers of sports or creative subjects', and that, when specialist teachers were used, the lack of connection with the main work of the school meant that 'talents were not systematically developed' (ibid., para. 89, p. 30).

The picture was similar in *EiC* secondary schools, with the talent area lagging behind provision for academically gifted pupils:

In most schools provision for gifted and talented pupils is developing well, although provision for talented pupils is not as well co-ordinated or as far advanced as that for gifted pupils.

(ibid., p. 54)

The report recommends that schools in *EiC* should specifically consider

improving the identification of talented pupils and making more consistent and planned provision for them.

(ibid., para. 255, p. 72)

This book addresses many of these issues, with a view to helping schools to identify and provide more effectively for their talented pupils – both those whose talents are evident, and those pupils with latent, undeveloped talents.

There is much evidence that involvement in the talent realm benefits *all* pupils, not just those with outstanding talents. Schools which are *talent enhancing* offer an enriched and enriching environment in which confidence and self-esteem flourish (see Chapters 9 and 10, 'The talent-enhancing school').

As a first step, some thought needs to be given to the nature of talent, and to some of our preconceptions about this area. Without a clear vision of what it means to be talented, how can we begin to identify talented pupils – particularly those whose talent is as yet undiscovered? And if we can't *discover* talent in our schools, how can we go on to *develop* it effectively and sensitively?

Current definitions/models of 'giftedness' and 'talent'

The area of giftedness and talent has been the subject of an increasing amount of attention over the past twenty years or so, as successive governments have increasingly turned their attention towards meeting the special needs of their gifted and talented pupils. The 1990s in particular also witnessed a significant rise in the amount of research on the function of the brain. Technical advances such as Positron Emission Tomography or PET (initially developed to aid in the diagnosis and treatment of brain tumours, and conditions such as schizophrenia and Alzheimer's) have enabled researchers to look more closely at the function of the brain, and its hemispheres, with a view to understanding more about human achievement.[1]

It is an exciting and vibrant area of scholarship, which is developing rapidly. However, as a result the literature can sometimes seem confusing, as one terminology and one taxonomy (classification system) overtakes another in rapid succession.

---

1 Professor John Geake of Oxford Brookes University has used PET to investigate the differences in brain structure between mathematically gifted boys and girls, with interesting results. Boys' mathematical understanding seems to by-pass the linguistic area of the brain, making it difficult for them to explain how they arrived at an answer. The NRICH (Mathematics Enrichment Online Mathematics Enrichment Club) website includes a report on this work: www.nrich.maths.org.uk (accessed April 2004).

A confusion of terms

For the general reader, looking up references to the term 'talent', either on the web or in print, results in a confusing picture. Even in countries with a long history of state-sponsored programmes for able pupils, there is often no agreement over the use of the terms 'giftedness' and 'talent'.

For example, in the United States – where formal programmes for gifted pupils were established as early as 1961[2] – the1993 United States Department of Education definition of talent includes both academic and non-academic fields:

> Children and youth with outstanding talent...exhibit *high performance capability in intellectual, creative, and/or artistic areas*, possess an unusual leadership capacity, or excel in specific academic fields...*Outstanding talents are present...in all areas of human endeavour.*
>
> (Quoted in Ofsted 2001a, footnote to p. 11; emphasis added)

Yet, in contrast, two American scholars (Ellen Winner and Gail Martino) began their article on 'Giftedness in non-academic domains' by stating:

> *It is common to distinguish between giftedness and talent.* Children who are advanced in scholastic abilities or have a high IQ are labelled gifted, while those who show exceptional ability in an art form or an athletic area are called talented.
>
> (Winner and Martino 2000, p. 95; emphasis added)

Even though Winner and Martino go on to argue that those with talent in an art form should also be termed 'gifted',[3] it's clear that a consensus has yet to be reached, and that in many people's minds, talent and giftedness relate to very different things.

Joan Freeman, in her book *Gifted Children Grown Up*, associates the term 'talent' with the creative arts, including poetry, and gives advice on 'techniques to develop talent', which include

> trying to recreate environments which have encouraged inspiration before...The most important thing is that the environment for creativity must be free as possible from anxiety...
>
> (Freeman 2001, p. 212)

This might prove a trifle confusing for an interested reader, looking for information on sport!

---

2   California established the first programmes for academically gifted students scoring in the 98th percentile or above on standardised intellectual ability tests, and in 1980 established one of the first GATE (Gifted and Talented Education) programmes to include those with high ability in the visual and performing arts.

3   There are some difficulties in applying Winner and Martino's conclusions to the performing arts (such as music and drama) and sport. See below, pp. 17–18.

A word about creativity

The word 'creativity' is often used in connection with the so-called 'Creative Arts' subjects: Music, Drama, Dance, Art & Design and, sometimes, Physical Education. However, this can be problematic since, as in the case of the terms 'giftedness' and 'talent', there is no commonly agreed definition for the term 'creativity'. In fact many writers would argue very strongly that **'creativity' can occur in any area, whether academic or non-academic.**

The Robinson Report (NACCCE 1999) entitled *All our Futures: Creativity, Culture and Education* (the foundation of much of the recent re-emphasis on creativity in our schools) clearly states that creativity is not just confined to the arts:

> Creativity is possible in all areas of human activity, including the arts, sciences, at work, at play and in all other areas of daily life. All people have creative abilities and we all have them differently.
>
> (p. 6)

Defining creativity as 'applied imagination', it links creativity with originality and, above all, with action:

> Creativity carries with it the idea of action and purpose...
>
> (*ibid.*, para. 30, p. 31)

> By creative education we mean forms of education that develop young people's capacities for original ideas and action...
>
> (*ibid.*, para. ii, p. 5)

At around the same time as the Robinson Report was being presented to the UK Government, Professor Robert Sternberg of Yale University (author of books such as *Thinking Styles* and *Intelligence, Heredity and Environment*) edited an important volume called the *Handbook of Creativity*, 'to provide the most comprehensive, definitive, and authoritative single-volume review available in the field of creativity' (Sternberg 1999, p. ix). Sternberg also sees creativity as a much broader concept, encompassing not only the arts, but science, business and society in general.

Again, linking the imaginative and the practical, he defines creativity as:

> the ability to produce work that is both novel (i.e., original, unexpected) and appropriate (i.e., useful, adaptive concerning task constraints).
>
> (Sternberg and Lubart 1999, p. 3)

He goes on to say that:

> Creativity is a topic of wide scope that is important at both the individual and societal levels for a wide range of task domains.
>
> (*ibid.*, p. 3)

In other words, creativity involves the conjunction of the original and unexpected, with the practical and useful (Figure 1.1).

As such it is equally relevant when applied to novelists, artists, entrepreneurs, scientists or chief executives.

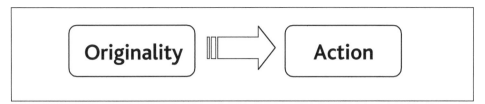

Figure 1.1

This makes sense. If we think of creative people as imaginative problem-solvers, applying original, imaginative solutions within the constraints of a particular situation, then a 'creative' footballer who gets his team out of a tight spot and a scientist who uses a new approach to solve an old problem are essentially the same. In the arts, a composer who works within the stylistic constraints of his time-period (e.g. Mozart) and yet expands the limits of expression can be regarded as particularly creative; in the same way that a dancer like Rudolf Nureyev expanded the role and range of expression for male ballet dancers. Likewise, an entrepreneur who launches a new product or takes over and transforms a failing company is showing the same kind of link between imagination and practicality.

So, in the end, the inclusion of the term 'creativity' in discussions of talent (in the DfES/*EiC* sense of the arts and sport) is something of a red herring; since it applies equally well to all domains, not just to the creative arts and sport.

Creative individuals

Yet it is true that the performing and visual arts (and, to a lesser extent, sport) have consistently placed a high value on creativity, especially in the context of its emphasis on invention and individuality, coupled with practical action. Certainly our expectations of successful individuals in the talent realm are coloured by our perceptions of what it means to be 'creative' or 'original' (e.g. that someone proficient in the visual arts might dress in an unconventional way).

Because these realms value originality, a young person beginning to explore his/her identity as an artist, a dancer, or a musician might well find themselves pushing the limits of what is expected in school, in terms of conventional behaviour. In the same way, a young footballer might mimic the off-field behaviour prevalent in leading players of the game. In fact their unconventional behaviour can be seen as a positive sign of increasing confidence and identification with their talent area; not a negative rebellion against authority.

Some writers have sought to define creativity by trying to characterise the personalities of creative individuals.

Although not particularly relevant to these discussions, my favourite of these descriptions is perhaps the simplest:

> a capacity for childlike wonder, carried into adult life, typifies the creative person.
>
> (Couger 1996, quoted in Morrison and Johnston 2003, p. 152)

Some definitions of 'talent'

A web search on the word 'talent' can bring up items as diverse as Civil Service staff development work, and discussions about 'developing talent' in the context of personnel management in business. In fact one writer has pointed out that there are currently over 200 different definitions of 'giftedness' and a proliferation of terms such as 'gifted', 'talented', 'more able' and so on (George 1997, p. 10). At times it can seem like a minefield. It is certainly useful to have some idea of the various definitions around, in order to avoid confusion.

Often termed 'models', some of the most frequent uses of the term 'talent' are:

1. Talent as 'natural ability', say, in a particular sport or activity, e.g. 'She has a talent for singing'.
2. Talent as a specific ability or strength in one particular area, e.g. a child with a 'particular talent for maths', rather than more generalised intellectual ability across a range of subjects.
3. Talents as gifts (natural abilities) which have been systematically developed through study, practice, etc. For instance, a child 'gifted' in sensorimotor skills might develop these in different ways, e.g. into a 'talent' for basketball, or swimming, or dance.
4. Talents as part of a range of natural abilities – or 'intelligences' – on a par with language or mathematical ability.

Nature versus nurture

What most of these have in common is the assumption that there is some such thing as 'innate ability', and that it is possible to identify it. For most of us, talent – particularly in the creative arts and sport – is something which is given mysteriously to people at birth: they have a genetic predisposition to their particular area of talent, which in time is 'bound to show'.

In fact, ability (in any area) can change and develop over time. Furthermore, there is now a range of research in the field of Expert Performance (see below, p. 22) which indicates that innate ability – even if it can be accurately measured – is not enough: that a major determinant of success – especially in the talent areas (as defined by the DfES) is the amount of time spent in purposeful practice, to develop these skills.

This is particularly important in the talent areas, which rely particularly heavily on physical skills developed over time, with training and practice.

Since all of these models and definitions are widely held, it is useful to look at them in more detail. In any case it is helpful to be familiar with some of the terminology used by specialists in the field.

Models and definitions based on 'nature'

1. Talent as 'natural ability'

This is probably the most prevalent use of the term 'talent' among the general public.

We often hear people speak of someone having a real 'talent' for an area, using the term virtually interchangeably with the word 'gift' – 'She has a real gift/talent for playing the piano' or 'He is a gifted/talented footballer'. In such cases both the word 'gift' and the word 'talent' mean the same thing: high natural (innate) ability. The unspoken assumption is that these talents will always show themselves, or that those who do not show talent straight away are not blessed with these abilities. Another assumption is that talents only 'run in families', or that talents are somehow 'effortless'.

Issues for schools: talent as 'natural ability'
Preconceptions about the nature of talent can colour teachers' perceptions of pupils' abilities and potential.

> **INSET**
> Working with colleagues, discuss some of your own experiences and ideas about the nature of talent. Is ability in music, art or sport innate and/or is it something which can develop over time? How might these views of talent affect teachers' attitudes to pupils?

2. Talent as specific, gifts as global

Writers on gifted education often use a rather different definition of 'gifts' and 'talents' – one which differentiates between the two terms. In this definition, a 'talented' person has exceptional abilities in one particular area/domain (e.g. in art, or maths). For those with abilities across a range of areas (those we might describe as 'all-rounders') the term is 'gifted' (see Figures 1.2 and 1.3).

The following is the terminology used by David George in his book, *The Challenge of the Able Child*:

> Having discussed at some length a definition of gifted and talented children, for the remainder of this book *I shall use the following working definition*: gifted students are those with a potential to exhibit superior performance across a wide range of areas of endeavour; talented students are those with a potential to exhibit superior performance in one area of endeavour.
>
> (1997, p. 18; emphasis added)

Although, under this model, a talented student might have strengths in one of the academic subjects, such as Maths or Modern Foreign Languages (MFL), and not necessarily in one of the creative arts, or sport, it has some similarities with the definition included in the *Ofsted Update 32* of Spring 2000:

Although an accurate definition is elusive, 'gifted' is usually taken to mean *a broad range of achievements at a very high level*, accompanied by very well developed learning skills. 'Talented' is usually taken to refer to one or more *specific talents*, such as sport or music, and not necessarily across all areas of the pupil's learning.

(Quoted by Frankie Williams in Eyre and Lowe 2002, p. 165)

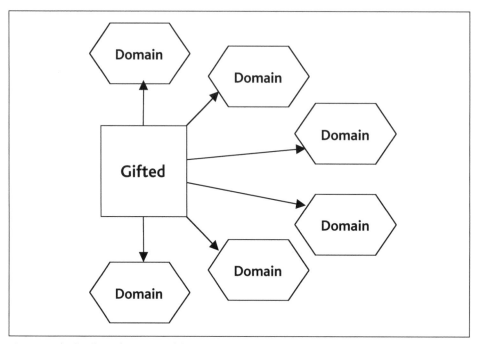

Figure 1.2 'Gifted' pupils: potential for superior performance in multiple domains

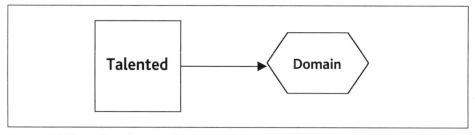

Figure 1.3 'Talented' pupils: potential for superior performance in one domain

Issues for schools: talents as specific, gifts as global

At first glance this seems a useful distinction. It's a very good descriptor of pupils who excel in only one academic area – say, creative writing, or maths, or science, or languages – yet who struggle in other areas of their school work.

The problem comes when we leap ahead to the assumption that 'talent' = something to do with the arts and sport.

We all know of youngsters who feel themselves to be 'useless' academically, yet who excel in sport, or in the arts. It can be dangerously tempting to 'deduce' from this that if you're really talented in one of these areas, you won't be 'academic'. This seriously disadvantages two groups:

- *Those with outstanding ability in the arts and sport, who use this as an excuse not to work hard at their academic subjects – with disastrous results in the long term, particularly if progress in their talent area is interrupted by injury.*
- *'All-rounders' who are strong academically, yet also have outstanding ability and a real passion for their talent area. They can come to feel under intense pressure to reject their 'non-academic' talents (see Chapter 6, 'Late developers and all-rounders').*

The idea that talented individuals will only have ability in one area is also based on a false premise: it's true that many of the outstanding individuals in the fields of sport and the arts are completely focused on their particular talent area, to the exclusion of other interests; but this may simply be because others with just as much potential made other, often agonised, choices about their careers.

3. Gagné: talents as 'developed gifts'

Other writers have defined the term 'talent' differently. In their view, 'giftedness' means *potential*, and 'talent' is *developed potential*. This definition seems to have originated with A. J. Tannenbaum. Writing in 1983 he suggested that:

> Keeping in mind that *developed talent* exists only in adults, a proposed definition of giftedness in children is that it denotes their *potential* for becoming critically acclaimed performers or exemplary producers of ideas in spheres of activity that enhance the moral, physical, emotional, social, intellectual, or esthetic life of humanity.
>
> (Tannenbaum 1983, p. 86, quoted in Gagné 1993, p. 70; emphasis added)

In its simplest form, then, the 'Talents as developed gifts' model looks like this:

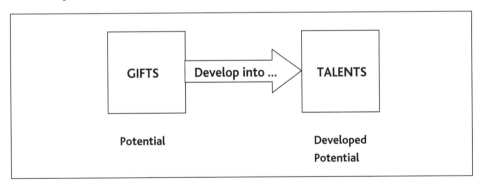

Figure 1.4

However, it is the work of Françoys Gagné (Professor of Psychology at the Université du Québec à Montréal) which is most closely associated with the definition of giftedness as *potential or innate ability*, and talent as *developed skills and knowledge*. This distinction between giftedness and talent has dominated gifted education, particularly in North America. As a result, many – but not all – American and Canadian publications in the field take as their basis Gagné's model. So it is worth taking a moment to become familiar with it.

Gagné's *Differentiated Model of Giftedness and Talent (DMGT)*

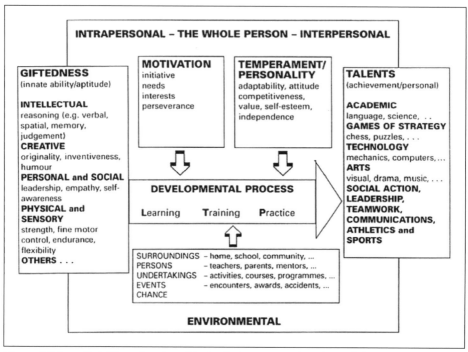

Figure 1.5 Gagné's *Differentiated Model of Giftedness and Talent (DMGT)* (Reprinted from *International Handbook of Giftedness and Talent*, 2nd edn, 2000, p. 68, Heller *et al.*, with permission from Elsevier)

Determined to differentiate in a systematic way between the terms 'giftedness' and 'talent', in his 1991 article 'Toward a differentiated model of giftedness and talent' Gagné put forward his own, much more elaborate model of talents as developed gifts (see Figure 1.5). In this model, 'Giftedness' consists of a series of *APTITUDE DOMAINS* which he calls *NATURAL ABILITIES (NAT)*:

- Intellectual
- Creative
- Socio-affective
- Sensorimotor
- Others (e.g. extrasensory perception).

These 'raw materials' of innate ability, may later develop (through what Gagné called the DEVELOPMENTAL PROCESS of Learning/Training/Practice) into systematically developed skills and knowledge in various fields of human endeavour. These he called FIELDS OF TALENT, or SYSTEMATICALLY DEVELOPED SKILLS (SYSDEV). Gagné himself described his model in this way:

> The Differentiated Model of Giftedness and Talent proposes a clear-cut distinction between the concepts of giftedness and talent. The term 'giftedness' designates the possession and use of untrained and spontaneously expressed natural abilities (called aptitudes or gifts) in at least one ability domain…By contrast, the term 'talent' designates the superior mastery of systematically developed abilities (or skills) and knowledge in at least one field of human activity…
>
> (Gagné 2000, p. 67)

> …in this model, natural abilities or aptitudes act as the 'raw materials'…of talents.
>
> (*ibid.*, p. 69)

Gagné's model turns the usual terminology on its head: talents – which most people think of as 'natural ability' – are not the starting point for development; instead they are the outcome of a **Developmental Process** which includes three elements:

■ *Learning,*

■ *Training* and

■ *Practice.*

Interpreting Gagné's model

There are several implications of this model, for those of us working in schools. For example, if gifts have to be developed in order to become talents, then we are unlikely to describe a young child as 'talented'. Talented individuals will for the most part be adults.

Looking more closely, there are also some difficulties in interpreting Gagné's model. For example, some activities do not fit comfortably into his categories:

■ What about dance? Would that come under Arts, or under Sports?

■ How does this model work with, say, 'artistic' forms of Technology, such as textiles?

■ Since video games require good hand–eye coordination and quick real-time responses, would they fit better with Sport than with more cerebral activities such as chess and puzzles?

Another difficulty is in the area of Learning, Training and Practice, which are essential elements in developing 'gifts' into 'talents'. The talent areas (in DfES terms, i.e. Music, Art, Drama, Sport, Dance) rely in varying but significant degrees on *physical skills* and *practice,* as opposed to theoretical *knowledge.* Physical skills differ fundamentally from knowledge in a number of ways, e.g. physical skills require expert coaching, and systematic and continued practice for their full development; whereas knowledge can be acquired independently of teaching/coaching (for example, through independent reading), and – in the absence of deterioration through illness or age – remains relatively constant.

While it is true that so-called 'academic skills' such as reading and essay-writing also improve with practice and regular use (and can become 'rusty'), there is no comparison between this and the amount of daily use and 'warming up exercises' required to keep a trumpet player's 'lip' in shape, or to ensure that a gymnast or dancer can express themselves flexibly, without injury.

This means that the balance between the three areas – *Learning, Training and Practice* – differs markedly between the more 'academic' subjects and those which are part of the talent area: in most of the academic subjects (and particularly in the more knowledge-based subjects) *Learning* is the major focus, underpinned by *Training* and *Practice*;[4] whereas in the talent areas *Training* and *Practice* play a much stronger role. For example, *learning* about Restoration comedy is only the first step in an actor's training: much time and effort then needs to go into *training* and *practice*, before the actor becomes an effective performer on stage.

Issues for schools

Gagné uses the term 'talent' in a distinctive way – a way which is the opposite of most people's understanding of the word. Since Gagné's views (in their various versions) have been so influential, and have been adopted by many other writers, it complicates the task of interpreting many of the writings on the topic of talent during the past decade.

4. Expanding the concept of intelligences: Goleman and Gardner

Both Daniel Goleman and Howard Gardner have been influential in seeking to expand the concept of 'ability' by identifying other areas of human potential which they argue are of equal importance. Goleman, in his best-selling book, *Emotional Intelligence* (1995), drew attention to what he termed 'emotional intelligence': an ability to sense and react to others in a way which made for success in life.

Gardner (initially in his *Frames of Mind: The Theory of Multiple Intelligences* (1983) and subsequently in a number of other books on the topic) has greatly expanded the list of potential human abilities, enabling a new perspective on the whole concept of 'ability' (see Figure 1.6). Using the term 'intelligences' to describe these abilities (which neatly side-steps the whole minefield of terminology surrounding the terms 'giftedness' and 'talent'!), Gardner – in his most recent refinement of his model – defines them as *areas of potential*:

---

4   Foreign languages require a heavier input of training and practice, and have more similarities with the talent areas.

Fundamentally, an intelligence refers to a biopsychological potential of our species to process certain kinds of information in certain kinds of ways.

(Gardner 1999, p. 94)

In Gardner's model, all human beings possess all of the 'intelligences', but in varying degrees. Over the course of a lifetime, different aspects are developed, depending on

the values of a particular culture, the opportunities available in that culture, and the personal decisions made by individuals and/or their families, schoolteachers, and others.

(*ibid.*, p. 34)

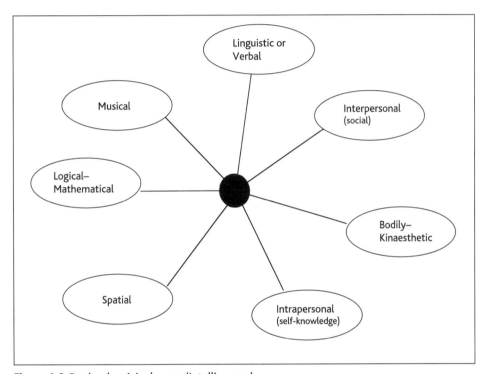

Figure 1.6 Gardner's original seven 'Intelligences'

Gardner's views have been taken up by a wide and enthusiastic group of followers, many of whom have attempted to apply his ideas to teaching and learning. In some cases these applications have been misguided or have confused Gardner's original theories, e.g. by attempting to devise 'tests' of the various intelligences. (Gardner began from the premise that testing – e.g. of IQ – was not productive.)

Issues for schools: all 'intelligences' are of equal value
Expanding the concept of intelligence to include areas such as musical, emotional and bodily–kinaesthetic aptitudes has been a significant development in our thinking about

human potential, and in particular about the talent areas. By widening the nature of what we think of as 'intelligence' the traditional hierarchy of 'academic' versus 'non-academic' subjects and pursuits suddenly disappears. Instead of some being 'more equal than others', all attributes – musical ability, linguistic ability, physical ability – are of equal value.

Gardner is firmly opposed to the subtle and continuing 'downgrading' of the 'non-academic' in preference to the 'academic':

> I am often asked whether an intelligence is the same thing as a talent or an ability...I have no objection if one speaks about eight or nine talents or abilities, but I do object when an analyst calls some abilities (like language) intelligences, and others (like music) 'mere' talents. *All should be called either intelligences or talents; an unwarranted hierarchy among the capacities must be avoided.*

(Gardner 1999, p. 83; emphasis added in final sentence)

Talent as 'natural ability'

All of the above models rely very heavily on the concept that human beings are endowed at birth with certain innate abilities; and with the underlying assumption that these abilities are the key to high performance. Yet the entire idea of innate or 'natural ability' is a complex one. Research has now shown that 'ability' is not a static thing, acquired at birth through genetic endowment and constant throughout life. Some researchers now dispute the whole concept of innate ability, and instead see it as something which develops through time, and in response to many different stimuli. In fact the term 'ability' is so problematic that many institutions (e.g. The Open University) have a 'house policy' to avoid using the word in course materials, substituting the more measurable concept of 'attainment'.

On the positive side, the work of Gardner and others has usefully (and in some cases, inspiringly) pointed out that 'natural ability' can be found in a whole range of areas, not just academic, but physical and emotional as well. This more holistic view has given a wider perspective on human potential and prompted a valuable rethinking of some of our assumptions about what is valuable in our society.

CHAPTER 2

'Academic' gifts and 'non-academic' talents

The DfES model of giftedness and talent

Having reviewed some of the other current definitions of the term 'talent', it is time to revisit our starting point: the DfES definition of 'talent'. The DfES definition makes a clear distinction between 'academic' gifts and 'non-academic' talents.[1]

'Gifted' pupils are those who show:

Ability in one or more subjects in the statutory school curriculum other than art, music and PE.

Whereas 'talented' pupils are:

Those with ability in art, music, PE or in any sport or creative art … and 'all-rounders'.

This straightforward model has a lot to recommend it:

- It is easily understood, since it corresponds closely with 'lay' definitions of the talent area.
- By linking the performing and visual arts and sport, it usefully highlights some areas which have much in common – i.e. an emphasis on physical skills, a heightened need for good coaching on a sustained basis, and a strong emotional element.
- The model makes a useful distinction between practical subjects based heavily on physical skills, and other subjects, which are more knowledge-based.

However, it also has some drawbacks:

- This definition does not correspond with many writers' definitions of 'talent' (see Chapter 1, 'What is talent?').

---

1   See the following DfES (2003) online publications: *Excellence in Cities: Further Guidance on the Gifted and Talented Strand; Information for Co-ordinators for the Gifted and Talented Pupil Cohort: Identification of the Gifted and Talented Pupil Cohort; Requirements for Schools to Identify Gifted and Talented Pupils* (www.standards.dfes.gov.uk).

- The phrase 'any sport or creative art' widens the potential scope of the talent area to the point where schools might find it difficult to decide which talents to recognise and support.
- It is not clear whether this definition includes other areas of the curriculum which also have a practical bias and an emphasis on developing physical skills, e.g. drama, design technology, MFL.
- There is a danger that emphasising the division of school subjects into 'academic' and 'non-academic' will lead to the arts and sport being considered 'second class'. (Of course, it might also have the opposite effect, and actually improve the standing of the so-called 'non-academic' subjects, by including them in considerations of 'high ability'.)

Certainly in the *Excellence in Cities* initiative (which has spearheaded so many developments in the education of gifted and talented pupils in England) the emphasis remains very strongly on those pupils with *academic* ability. Of the pupils on the register of gifted and talented pupils, 'those with academic ability, including "all-rounders", should form at least two-thirds of the cohort in each year group'.

This emphasis on the academic side is not surprising: an important aim of *Excellence in Cities* was to raise academic achievement and aspirations in deprived areas of England. However, by insisting that the academically able should form 'at least two-thirds of the cohort' it may have inadvertently contributed to the undervaluing of pupils' 'non-academic' talents.

In any case, in England the DfES's definition looks likely to remain the norm.

Issues for schools
Dividing the school curriculum into two distinct areas – the talent area for art, music and PE, the academic area for 'everything else' – creates some practical issues for schools:

- *The phrase 'any sport or creative art' means that the talent area potentially includes a bewilderingly wide range of activities, many of which are not part of the school curriculum at all. A pupil might be performing at a high level in ballet, through study taking place entirely outside school; or involved seriously in ice-skating or swimming or golf, through a club in the community. How do we then identify these pupils, and to what extent can we – should we – be providing support?*
- *By insisting that the academically able should form 'at least two-thirds of the cohort of each year group' a clear hierarchy is implied: that somehow academic achievement and potential are of more value than achievement and potential in the talent realm. This denies the importance of the talent areas in contributing to pupils' self-esteem and confidence (and as we know, all pupils thrive when their self-esteem and confidence are high); and ignores the increasing body of evidence that involvement in a talent area can increase pupils' academic achievements as well. (See Chapter 3, 'The talent area: benefits for pupils'.)*

Giftedness and talent: is there a difference?

Some authors have questioned the entire concept of distinguishing between 'academic' gifts and 'non-academic' talents, arguing that there is really no difference between the two. Ellen Winner and Gail Martino studied the characteristics of prodigiously gifted young visual artists, and identified three things they seemed to share with academically gifted children:

1. *precociousness* – they all showed signs of high ability early in childhood
2. they were *intensely motivated, with an obsessive interest in their work*
3. they showed a tendency to *march to their own drummer* – 'They learn virtually on their own, requiring minimum adult scaffolding, and often solve problems in their domain in novel, idiosyncratic ways'.

(Winner and Martino 2003, p. 335)

Martino and Winner's views have won wide acceptance among scholars and other writers. However, their findings do not apply quite so easily to some of the other talent areas.

Precociousness

Their work focused on art – and on drawing in particular. This is an area where *access* is not an issue: anyone can pick up a pen or pencil and draw. The training all children receive in learning to write transfers directly to handling a pen or pencil for drawing creatively; and art forms a significant part of the curriculum from preschool onwards. Studies show that primary school teachers, in particular, tend to feel fairly confident about teaching art to their classes (whereas in music, they are significantly less confident). As a result, precocious development in art is at least a possibility for nearly every youngster.

In the other talent areas, access is a real issue: although some pianists are self-taught, and can express themselves through their playing, without sustained access to a piano and lessons, very few children will show precocious talent in this area.

CASE STUDY

David is a locksmith, who runs a successful small business in a large city in the Midlands. Now in his forties, he attended a boys' secondary modern school, where music lessons consisted of a combination of classroom singing and listening to recordings. There were no instrumental music lessons available at his school, and his parents were not in a position to arrange for private lessons. Not a confident singer, David took no part in any school musical activities. In his teens, the family acquired an old upright piano (inherited from his grandmother). He loved the piano and set about teaching himself to play, using a book he borrowed from the local library.

David now owns his own grand piano, and a home recording studio, where he composes music for his own enjoyment. When he visited my home to replace a door lock, he asked if he could try out my piano, ably sight-reading a difficult Bach Prelude. His ten-year-old young son is already a confident pianist who is working on his Grade 2 examination, and improvising jazz.

No one can deny David's talent for music. One can not help but wonder what would have happened if he had had access to a piano and lessons at an early age.

The question of precocious development alone as an indicator of high ability is also problematic in other talent areas: since some physical skills can not be taught until later on in adolescence, we are unlikely to find a 'prodigy' in pole-vaulting or the hammer throw. Or in tuba playing.[2] But this does not mean that excellence and outstanding potential do not exist in these fields.

Intense motivation

Talented pupils do tend to be intensely motivated in their talent area. However, in a school context we are dealing with a whole range of pupils:

- those whose ability has been recognised and nurtured;
- those who have not yet been exposed to the coaching and training needed to reveal their abilities;
- underachievers, whose attainment has been hindered by a range of factors, including lack of confidence, difficult home circumstances, or simply the pressure of too many other activities;
- pupils who have been pressured unduly by parents, teachers or coaches, and have lost their motivation through 'burn out';
- pupils who care so deeply about their talent area that they are afraid to risk failure by showing how motivated they really are (see Chapter 5, pp. 49–51).

In considering Martino and Winner's findings, it is also important to remember some significant contrasts between the visual arts and the other talent areas.

Music performance, drama and sport take place in 'real time' and require continuous training, warming up and so on for the appropriate muscle memory and reflexes to be in peak condition. Since performers in these areas have to 'deliver the goods' under pressure, the preparation – warming up, training, etc. – take on a particular importance. Art (like musical composition and creative writing) is a more reflective activity, which may account for some of its similarity with more 'academic' pursuits. Few mathematicians have to do their work on a particular day or time or

---

2   One reason that violin prodigies are relatively common is simply that there are tiny violins available. Before smaller C clarinets became common (to enable younger pupils to begin the clarinet earlier) there were no prodigies in clarinet playing. The clarinet prodigy Julian Bliss began his studies at the age of four, on a (plastic) C clarinet.

place; whereas preparation for a performance or competition is the very essence of the performing arts and sport.

The range and scope of 'non-academic' talents

Since the range of talents pupils might display can seem almost limitless, in the case of the talent area the first task is to clarify which activities are relevant in the context of a particular school.

In the case of primary schools, the list of activities can be quite general, e.g. a pupil who is particularly agile in a range of playground games, or physical education activities. Or it can be very specific, e.g. pupils may already be seriously committed to highly specific activities such as Irish dancing, competitive swimming, or learning to play a musical instrument.

By secondary school, the areas have multiplied in line with pupils' growing expertise. Secondary school pupils may have a particular talent for playing the electric guitar or the oboe; or have specific skills such as jazz improvisation. In sport, by secondary school, talent is beginning to show in areas not covered by the primary school curriculum, e.g. throwing a javelin or competitive wrestling. In art, secondary school brings a wider range of skills and potential areas in which to excel: a pupil whose drawing skills in primary school were not outstanding might well find his or her niche in digital art forms, or in sculpture. New areas of expression come to the fore as well, including video production, music technology and a range of other creative outlets.

Talents developed outside school

Since many talents are developed outside school, another issue is the extent to which schools might be expected to identify and support pupils with these talents. Some schools have been very proactive in this, e.g. on discovering that a talented athlete (who was training entirely in a club in the community) was unable to move to the senior division in her sport because her family couldn't afford the necessary kit, the school arranged to purchase the kit with funds from the gifted and talented programme. At first sight this seems laudable: a needy pupil and an understanding school. However, this approach can lead to difficulties.

A hierarchy of talents?

Some schools are willing to support pupils involved in certain types of activities outside school, but may not have a considered policy regarding which activities are worthy of support. If the school is buying the kit for an outstanding athlete training in a private club, should the school also be providing bassoon reeds for a talented pupil? What about ballet shoes? Or boxing gloves? Unless a school has a definite policy regarding financial support of activities outside school (perhaps based on financial need, or on the achievement and potential of the individual involved), it is possible to inadvertently create a hierarchy of 'worthy' activities. This can have a demotivating effect on pupils whose outside activities are *not* receiving any financial support from the school.

Some possible talents

As a first step towards developing a policy regarding talented pupils, it can be useful simply to list the areas we think of as involving 'talent'. Since so many talents are developed primarily outside the school curriculum, through private tuition, clubs, classes and through the school's own extracurricular programme, it is important to include as wide a range as possible; for example:

- DJ-ing
- Painting
- Digital art
- Ice-skating
- Skateboarding
- Gymnastics
- Musical instrument/voice – classical, jazz and pop
- Football
- Off-road sports, e.g. moto-cross
- Computer games
- Judo
- Boxing
- Textiles
- Architecture
- Design (in its widest sense)
- Dance – classical ballet; modern dance; jazz; popular; Irish folk dancing.

INSET

- What areas of talent do we regard as 'acceptable': (a) as individuals; (b) in the context of our school? Take as an example various forms of dance: folk dancing; classical ballet; tap dancing; ballroom dancing; popular dance forms.
- How might schools support talented pupils whose training primarily takes place outside school, e.g. by celebrating their achievements in school assemblies?
- Is it appropriate for schools to provide financial help for pupils whose training is taking place outside school? If decisions have to be made, what criteria might be used, e.g. time devoted to the activity, level of attainment, matching the ethos of the school and so on?
- What is your school's policy on releasing pupils from school to attend events and competitions which are not arranged through school?

Skills development and Expert Performance

Skills versus knowledge

One thing that these varied talents have in common is that they are primarily *skills-based*, as opposed to *knowledge-based*. In other words, talents such as ice-skating, singing, drawing and so on are not the sorts of things we learn to do simply by reading a book, or hearing someone talk about them. They are *skills*, which require regular use and practice to master.

In contrast, *knowledge* is something which we can often grasp the first time around. We can read an article about some new development in, say, solar energy; and although we may have to re-read the article a couple of times if we are unfamiliar with the concepts and terms used, in the end, once we understand what it is about, we *know* it. Until such time as we forget it, we don't have to *practise* that knowledge, and we do not necessarily have to apply it to something.

So the process of acquiring knowledge and the process of acquiring skills are not the same.

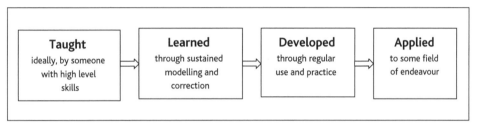

Figure 2.1 Skills acquisition

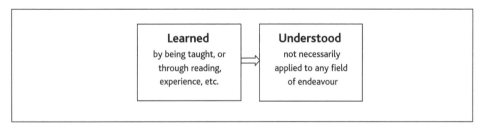

Figure 2.2 Knowledge acquisition

The models represented in Figures 2.1 and 2.2 are fundamentally different.

In *skills development* the role of the **teacher/coach** and the importance of **regular use and practice** makes for a much more extended process. This is particularly the case for **physical skills**, which characterise the talent area. Good teaching is important to learning in every area, but particularly so in sport, dance and music, where the physical skills involved require regular modelling and constant correction in order to establish the technique needed to reach the highest levels of performance.

Muscle memory is so persistent that poor coaching and poor technique can seriously hamper progress and, in some cases, cause injury. (This is why adjudicators of dance competitions are particularly strict about technique: if poor teaching results in consistently poor technique, youngsters can literally be 'damaged for life'.)

Physical skills and talents

The talent area is typified by the development of *physical skills*. Drama requires skills in speaking and stage movement; the visual arts involve a range of skills, from drawing to computer graphics to textiles; musicians need general skills in musicianship, coupled with highly developed skills in their particular area (performance, composition, etc.); sports men and women couple high levels of general fitness with expertise in particular activities, from swimming to gymnastics to rugby. These skills are first *developed*, and then applied. For example, professional dancers face a gruelling routine of daily exercises in order to be able to express themselves through their art form.

This means that most talent areas require:

1. **a level of general fitness**, maintained by regular training, e.g. a footballer jogging to build stamina and endurance, a French horn player playing long notes every day to 'keep the lip in', an artist 'keeping their hand in' by regular use of a particular medium;
2. **skills development**, requiring expert coaching linked with *practice*, e.g. a swimmer learning a new stroke, a pianist practising scales, a singer learning how to sing high notes comfortably, a drama student working towards examinations in speech.

Issues for schools

■ *Talented pupils will need the time, equipment and facilities required to establish and maintain fitness.*
■ *They will need expert coaching to avoid developing bad habits, and to reach their full potential. In many cases, this coaching will only be available outside school.*

Expert Performance: 'Practice, practice and more practice'

How do you get to Carnegie Hall? Practice, practice and more practice.

(Anonymous)

Carnegie Hall in New York City is a well-known venue for young artists to make their debuts as solo performers. There's an old joke where someone is late for a concert there, and is wandering around the streets of New York, looking for Carnegie Hall. He approaches a passer-by and asks, 'How do I get to Carnegie Hall?' Naturally, the reply is: 'Practice, practice and more practice!'

The development of expertise through purposeful practice – also known as the development of **Expert Performance** – has come in for a great deal of attention from scholars and coaches over the past decade or so.

Nature versus nurture: the great debate

Writers such as K. Anders Ericsson (in sport) and John Sloboda (in music) have made an important contribution to the eternal debate on 'nature versus nurture' by arguing that the essence of high achievement in a range of fields is mainly attributable to 'practice, practice and more practice' (Ericsson 1996, Sloboda 1996, and elsewhere).

This work has arisen partly as a reaction against the view that abilities are genetically determined. In this view – still held by many in the general population – gifts and talents are inherited: if you haven't got 'it' at birth, you'll never have 'it'.

In the case of musical talent, Sloboda feels that there is a mistaken, 'folk psychology of talent', according to which

> few people become expert musical performers because few people have the necessary talent.
>
> (Sloboda 1996, p. 108)

Sloboda goes on to say that in a recent survey 'more than 75% of a sample...believed that composing, singing, and playing concert instruments required a special gift or natural talent'.

Along with his team at Keele University, Sloboda studied five groups of students, ranging from those who had attained places at highly specialised music schools (such as Chetham's, or the Yehudi Menuhin School) by competitive audition, to those who had begun to learn an instrument but had given up. He found that 'deliberate, purposeful practice' was the main factor in their success – not some supposedly innate and mysterious 'talent'. With his fellow researchers, he found that the high-achieving players had put in something like 10,000 hours of purposeful practice to achieve their goals.

High achievement arises from a whole range of factors, including genetic characteristics, parental support, good teaching and practice! It is clear that both nature *and* nurture are involved. Sloboda's research has been very influential in modifying the view that talent is entirely determined by 'innate ability', by highlighting the role of personal effort (often supported by families who encouraged students to carry on practising consistently) in achieving success as a performer.

Practice as the key to 'success' in the talent realm

It is worth remembering, though, that by identifying as 'successful' those students who had attained places at specialist music colleges, the underlying assumption is that the others – who included a group that he described as 'playing for pleasure' – as 'failures'. This is a general failing which takes as its starting point of research successful athletes, musicians and scientists, and 'work backwards' by analysing the elements of their success.

- What about those who gained a great deal from their studies but did not go on to play (or act, or compose, or design) professionally? (See Chapter 4, 'Redefining success'.)

- What about the underachievers, who did *not* do the requisite practice? How can we unlock their latent talent, and encourage them to put in the necessary hours to fulfil their potential?

- What about those who *did* put in the hours, but weren't successful at the highest levels?

- Specialist music schools have very strict and demanding practice regimes. There is a relatively high 'burn out' rate in conservatoires for students from specialist music schools. Did the hours of practice take their toll in terms of students' long-term development?

Practice makes perfect: general principles of Expert Performance

- High achievement is related to *long-term development of skills and knowledge* – generally a span of about ten years.

- The key to success is *'deliberate, purposeful practice'* – e.g. in writing about sport, Ericsson distinguishes between 'play' and 'practice'.

- Expert Performance is a concept which applies to *all fields*, i.e. not just sport and the arts.

Renzulli's three-ring conception of giftedness

The American academic, Joseph Renzulli, has also created a model for high performance which takes account of deliberate effort as an important element in high achievement (again, in any field, not just in the arts and sport). His *Three-ring Conception of Giftedness* sees the source of high achievement as a *combination* of three factors:

- **higher than average ability** (i.e. not 'outstanding' ability, or even 'high' ability)
- **creativity**
- **task commitment**.

In Renzulli's view, all three need to be present for an individual to reach the highest possible levels of achievement. His model has become one of the most influential in the field of gifted and talented education.

Issues for schools

- *Even if schools are unable to provide expert coaching, they can still play an important role in fostering task commitment and creating an environment in which creativity can flourish.*
- *Schools can also inadvertently undermine pupils' task commitment, e.g. by allowing the 'star pupil' to take a leading role when they haven't attended rehearsals regularly. (Chapters 9 and 10, 'The talent-enhancing school', describe some practical strategies for building task commitment.)*

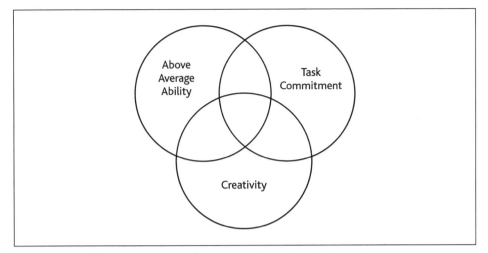

Figure 2.3 Renzulli's three-ring model

Task commitment and talent development

Renzulli, Sloboda and Ericsson all see high performance as the result of personality traits as well as 'natural gifts'. In their view, hard work is just as important as 'native ability' in achieving potential.

In fact, those with high 'natural ability' may ultimately be at a disadvantage. Because things come easily to them, they may not develop the necessary task commitment to see them through when the inevitable challenges arise.

The ballet dancer Sylvie Guillem has been described as 'one of the most brilliant and exciting – and one of the highest paid – dancers of the twentieth century'. The daughter of a gymnastics teacher, Sylvie initially trained as a gymnast, before discovering her potential for ballet at the age of 11, during an exchange programme with the Paris Opera Ballet School. By the age of 19, she had progressed to the highest level of her profession. (Her move to London's Royal Ballet in 1989 caused such an outcry in France that the culture minister had to answer questions on the topic in the National Assembly!)

Speaking in 1993, she gave a performer's view of the importance of task commitment in developing talent:

> I'm not like this just because it's a gift. I was lucky to have [a] gift, I admit! But I worked a lot. And this is difficult for everybody – to work.
>
> And it's also difficult when you have [a] gift – to know that you have to work and to understand it. Because it's all so easy to stop where you are and just to use the gifts you have. [But that] doesn't give good things at the end.
>
> You must use all of that. It's ingredients, you know. If you don't use them well, you have not a good cake or not a good something to eat.

> (Bragg *et al.* 1993)

The talent area: benefits for pupils

Introduction: the status of the arts and sport within the curriculum

Art, music and physical education have formed part of the curriculum in English schools almost from the beginning. Yet there have always been issues surrounding their importance in pupils' education, and the status of these areas within schools. The perpetual tension between those who feel that academic subjects are the main focus of school life, and those who emphasise the importance of a balanced curriculum is one outcome of these underlying issues.

These tensions are nothing new. Perhaps best known for its championing of 'child-centred' education, the 1967 Plowden Report on *Children and their Primary Schools* (DES 1967) provided a unique snapshot of the state of art, music and PE in English primary schools at that time. The Report is very clear about the importance of the 'non-academic' subjects. Here are its comments about art:

> Art is both a form of communication and a means of expression of feelings which ought to permeate the whole curriculum and the whole life of the school. A society which neglects or despises it is dangerously sick. It affects, or should affect, all aspects of our life from the design of the commonplace articles of everyday life to the highest forms of individual expression.
>
> (para. 676, p. 247)

The Report acknowledged that good work was taking place, but expressed some concerns over the full development of art in schools. Some of these concerns sound very familiar, e.g. worries about non-specialist teachers' lack of confidence in supporting pupils' development in this area (still very much an issue today). However, it also touches on the broader question of status of art within the curriculum and within the school:

> A more fundamental obstacle to full development is the lukewarm attitude not only of the public but also of many teachers and many schools, especially academically selective grammar schools, to the importance of art in education. If the word 'frill' is not now often used of it, the attitude that it implies is still widespread.
>
> (*ibid.*, para. 680, p. 249)

In other words the more 'academic' the school, the less value was given to the creative arts.

Sadly, the world described in the Plowden Report is not entirely a thing of the past. There are still some highly academic schools where the status of the creative arts and sport remains that of an 'add on' or 'frill', competing unsuccessfully for pupils' time and attention.

Even in schools which see the arts and sport as important parts of the curriculum, too often the underlying attitude regards them as 'polite accomplishments' to make for a 'well-rounded individual'; whereas an increasing body of evidence is showing that involvement in the talent areas can confer a whole range of benefits, including academic success. In fact the 'non-academic' talent areas are increasingly being recognised not only as fundamental to pupils' overall development, but also as significant contributors to teaching and learning.

Hopefully the new wave of Specialist Secondary Schools (which now include Art, Sports, Music and Performing Arts) should help to raise the standing of these subjects in the eyes of parents, pupils and staff alike. This can only be to the good.

A range of benefits

A number of research findings indicate that involvement in sport and in the creative arts can have significant positive effects on pupils' overall development. The benefits can occur in a whole range of areas, including:

- **Cognitive development and academic achievement**
- **Physical development** – both fitness and general health
- **Emotional well-being** – especially confidence, self-esteem and identity
- **Social skills** – such as teamwork and loyalty.

Cognitive development and academic achievement

In terms of research into connections between academic achievement and the talent areas, music is the talent area which has received the most attention.

Cognitive development

There are many studies linking musical skills to different aspects of cognitive development. For example, a recent study found that young children who had received music lessons showed improved test scores in spatial reasoning (Rauscher *et al.* 1997) . Another study (from Hong Kong) showed significant improvement in verbal memory in boys aged 5–15 who, over a five-year period, were given lessons in playing classical music on Western instruments; which suggests that music stimulates the left side of the brain (which controls verbal reasoning). When boys stopped having the lessons, the improvement in verbal learning stopped.

Academic achievement

Professor James Catterall and his colleagues in the 'Imagination Project' at the University of California at Los Angeles (UCLA) have looked at the wider issue of involvement in the arts (in this case, both music and drama/theatre arts) and academic achievement (Catterall *et al.* 1999). Over a ten-year period they followed the progress of more than 25,000 American High School students whom they described as 'arts involved'. In these students (ranging in age from 13 to 18) they found very strong evidence of the effects of their involvement in instrumental music and drama, whether inside school or in extracurricular activities.

Students who were engaged in the arts on a regular basis were consistently linked to academic success. In Mathematics, students with high levels of involvement in instrumental music 'show significantly higher levels of mathematics proficiency' by the time they leave school. Theatre arts students, on the other hand, showed development in other areas, including:

> Gains in reading proficiency, gains in self concept and motivation, and higher levels of empathy and tolerance for others.
>
> *(ibid.,* p. 1)

The key to this is *sustained* involvement. In the case of drama students, this was defined as 'acting in plays and musicals, participating in drama clubs, and taking acting lessons'. Musicians were those who were involved in instrumental lessons and performing groups, both inside and outside school. These are *long-term* gains, arising from a *long-term commitment* to a talent area.

Socio-economic status, the arts and academic achievement

An interesting feature of the UCLA study is its discovery that the gains involved in arts involvement were *independent of social class.* In general, middle-class children have many more opportunities for exposure to and involvement in the arts. This is borne out by research data which shows that the probability of 'high arts' involvement is almost twice as high for those from advantaged families (*ibid.,* p. 3). Conversely, the probability of 'low arts' involvement is about twice as high, for students from economically disadvantaged families (*ibid.,* p. 11).[1]

Catterall and his colleagues decided to look at the data after eliminating social class as a factor. They found that 'arts involved' students from lower socio-economic groups showed the same academic benefits (higher academic achievement, staying on in school and better attitudes) as those from well-off families. In fact the results were striking: low-income students involved in instrumental music were twice as likely to achieve high levels in mathematics than the 'low arts' students.

This argues very strongly for the importance of talent identification and support programmes, particularly in areas of high socio-economic advantage.

---

1   In students of low-economic status: of those in the 'No Music' group, 15.5 per cent achieved high levels in maths; in the 'High Music' group, the figure was 33.1 per cent.

Physical education, sport and academic achievement

There is a commonly held view that sports men and women are less able academically. This stereotype – which often goes along with the view that if a pupil is weak at academic subjects he/she will automatically be good at practical ones – is based on a false premise: a kind of skewed idea of 'fairness', where 'everyone has their strengths', so those who struggle academically must be blessed with abilities in another sphere. As a kind of 'mirror image', academically able pupils are typically portrayed (in the UK, at least) as bespectacled and awkward, particularly in sport.

Unfortunately this charitable view of the distribution of gifts and talents is not supported by the facts! High ability pupils are just as capable at physical education as their less able counterparts. In fact many of our high-achieving pupils in our schools tend to be good across the board (see Chapter 6, 'Late developers and all-rounders').

Although the findings are not as clear-cut as they are with the arts, physical education and sport have also been identified as contributing both to cognitive development and to academic achievement.

Regarding specific links between **cognitive development** and physical education, the Institute of Youth Sport at Loughborough University has reviewed the research literature and come to the conclusion that

> there is some support for a link between physical education, motor/movement skill learning and a correlation with cognitive development.
>
> (Institute of Youth Sport 2001a, p. 19)

In particular, specific research on motor/movement skill learning and motor activity has shown a correlation with academic areas such as reading, mathematics and language.

At the very least, studies show that for pupils engaged in physical education and sport, academic performance does not *suffer* as a result of reduced academic study time.

In 2001, the Qualifications and Curriculum Authority (QCA) launched its **Physical Education and School Sport Investigation (PESS)**, commissioned jointly by the DfES and the Department for Culture, Media and Sport. The aim was twofold:

- to explore ways of improving the quality of PE and school support;
- to investigate the difference that high-quality PE and school sport can make to young people and their schools.

Their findings have provided some first-hand information about the benefits for pupils of high-quality PE and school sport.

Overall, they found that:

> Schools with good records in PE and school sport report higher attainment in PE among pupils, as might be expected, but also *higher achievement across the curriculum.*
>
> (QCA 2001; emphasis added)

Test results in the schools were felt to be higher as a result of pupils being fit, active and motivated. Schools with high participation rates in sport also reported lower truancy rates and better behaviour.

Physical development

Physical education, sport and dance have clear benefits for pupils, in terms of their physical development, fitness and general health.

We live in an era when children in Western Europe are increasingly at risk of a whole range of chronic illnesses, including heart disease, as a result of a sedentary lifestyle. Regular participation in PE, sport and dance while at school can help to counteract the effects of hours of video games and television watching. If a youngster becomes seriously involved in sport or dance, the hours spent in training are hours spent away from the computer screen. Although there are some concerns about the effects of ballet training – and, in particular, overly strict dieting regimes – in general, physical activities are 'a good thing' for pupils.

Habits of physical exercise established in primary and secondary school predispose to continuing with those activities in later life. It is not at all uncommon these days to see men and women in their fifties who are still actively involved in team sports.

Pupils who are involved in the arts can also reap benefits. Again, time spent in rehearsals is time spent away from the television set or the computer game console. Researchers for the UCLA 'Imagination Project' also noted significantly less time spent in television watching by its 'arts involved' students, with a much higher proportion watching one hour or less of television per week (Catterall *et al.* 1999, p. 3).

Emotional well-being

Participation in a talent area can make a tremendous difference to a student's emotional well-being and sense of self-esteem.

Confidence – Creating work and then presenting it to others (as a work of art, as a performance or in the context of a competition) can be a daunting experience. Pupils who overcome their fears mature and grow in self-confidence. Since many talent activities are undertaken in teams/groups, for youngsters who are less confident they can provide an opportunity for shared experiences. Progression is possible, with pupils gradually gaining in confidence as they progress from understudy to a minor role to a leading actor, from singer in the chorus to soloist, from third chair trumpet to first, from substitute to playing regularly in the team.

Identity – As pupils develop their interest and skills in an activity, they begin to see themselves as 'dancers', 'musicians', 'footballers', 'actors'. This process of identification generally begins with identification with a group, e.g. 'I'm a member of the band'. It may go on to involve dressing in a particular way, enjoying spending time in certain areas of the school (e.g. the art room, or the music practice area), attending artistic/sporting events outside school, developing a new vocabulary associated with the talent area. This sense of identity can be an important focus of self-esteem, particularly in the teen years.

Emotional expression and physical release – The National Foundation for Educational Research (NFER) Report *Arts Education in Secondary Schools: Effects and Effectiveness* (Harland *et al.* 2000) speaks of the 'heightened sense of enjoyment, excitement, fulfilment and therapeutic release of tensions' gained by pupils involved in the arts (p. 1). The talent areas (including sport) provide a vital means of emotional expression. The strong physical element in drama, music performance and sport can also serve as an important outlet for aggression, anger and tension.

> ### CASE STUDY
>
> James joined my GCSE Music class late in the Summer Term of Year 10. Then aged 15, he had been suspended from school for the whole of the previous two terms, and had a reputation for lashing out angrily at other students who teased him. By this time he had missed nearly three full terms of study. To complicate matters, he didn't read music, and didn't have a performing instrument! Fortunately he had a good singing voice, and over the next term he was gradually drawn into a high-profile singing group within the school. He began to have lessons in singing, and in time used his singing talent to achieve well in the Performing component of GCSE Music.
>
> I never saw his legendary temper. There was never a tantrum in a music lesson, or in the music area, where he increasingly came to find a haven. Several members of the singing group were popular and successful in the wider school community. As his confidence increased, they became his friends and colleagues. Gradually, his isolation within his year group faded into the past, and at the end of Year 11 he performed in a school concert as part of a pop band, singing very movingly as a soloist – proud to be 'one of the group'. Bolstered by the confidence gained progressively through performing – first in a large group, then in the smaller singing group, and finally as a soloist – his image in the school and his image of himself changed utterly.
>
> His academic work in other subjects was also transformed, and he stayed on into the sixth form, a confident, competent young man.

Social skills

James's story highlights another important element which benefits pupils who are committed to an area of talent: the development of social skills and, in particular, teamwork. Although some talent areas are solitary (e.g. training as a solo pianist), in many activities the shared experience of training and preparing for concerts and competitions helps to build team spirit. Even in individual sports such as athletics or boxing, training generally takes place in the context of a club or team: the emphasis may be on 'solo' performance, but the approach is still a team effort. And anyone who has ever participated in a theatrical performance knows that performers and stage-hands alike form a very close-knit team by the end of the run.

A team approach offers a number of benefits:

- It provides a **range of roles** – not everyone needs to take a leading role. This allows for differentiation in terms of interests, skills and temperaments; and widens potential participation.

- It involves a sense of **shared endeavour** – success and failure alike are shared by the team members. When difficulties arise, team-mates can provide support and encouragement. In fact it has been suggested that one reason boys seem to cope with failure better than girls is their experience of predominantly team-based sports. When the inevitable mistakes come in training and in the game itself, boys have the support of their team-mates saying, 'Don't worry. Better luck next time', etc. This experience of 'supported failure' is a good preparation for life.

- It fosters skills in **collaboration and co-operation** – important elements in working in any environment – providing an opportunity to practise and develop them on a regular basis.

- It helps to build and reinforce **task commitment**, e.g. pupils who participate regularly in ensembles are more likely to continue playing musical instruments throughout their school careers. The sense of loyalty to a widened friendship group helps to sustain interest and involvement.

Working together on a project – a concert, a sporting event, an exhibition, a design, a play or musical – is the best possible preparation for project-based work in adult life.

Talent development and task commitment

The overall benefits of a sustained commitment to a talent area are therefore significant. Some of these benefits are highly specific to the particular talent, e.g. youngsters who excel at sport develop their large motor skills to a high level, singers and players of wind instruments learn to manage their breathing well, visual artists have highly developed appreciation of colour, texture and layout, drama students have more empathy for people from different walks of life and of different races. However, some of the benefits – such as improved academic achievement – do not seem so closely related to a specific talent area.

Since these benefits seem to be associated with *sustained* involvement with a talent area, one reason may be related to an increase in pupils' **task commitment**. In Chapter 2 ('"Academic" gifts and "non-academic" talents') we looked briefly at the work of Joseph Renzulli, who highlighted the importance of task commitment as an element in high achievement (see Figure 3.1).

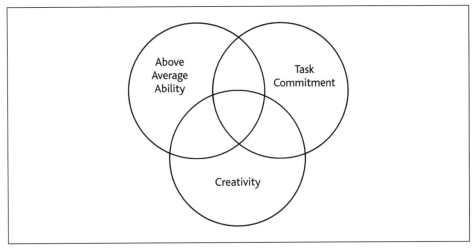

Figure 3.1 Renzulli's three-ring model

Success in any of the talent areas (indeed, in every area of life!) requires perseverance and resilience, reliability and dedication. These skills are transferable to other aspects of life. This does not mean that every pupil with a keen interest in sport or the arts is going to be the most dedicated student in other subjects! Quite the contrary. In fact they may be so dedicated to the one area that other work is not given the priority it needs (see Chapter 8, 'Talented pupils'). But in the long term, they have learned how to *work*, and along with this, they have learned how to accept mistakes, take risks and persevere. Many will also have learned how to work as part of a team towards shared goals. Once a pupil has tasted the success of working in the *long term* towards a goal, in the face of set-backs, distractions and discouragement, he/she has learned a vital lesson about life.

Creativity and risk-taking

To be a creative person means to be willing to take risks and try out new ideas and ways of looking at things. In order to do this, we need 'permission' to make mistakes, to fail and then to try again.

What does a commitment to a talent area involve, at every level? From the very first, there is struggle involved: the struggle to master the skills needed for self-expression and success. And since the outcomes are so public (art is displayed, sport is openly competitive, dance and the other performing arts eventually involve an audience or an examiner hearing/seeing and responding to our efforts), the pressure is unique.

This struggle can take many forms:

- A primary school pupil struggling to master the skills required in drawing and painting; a college student learning to use a computer program to express himself in digital art forms.

- A teenager trying to memorise his first big dramatic role in a play; a Year 3 pupil practising a poem to read in assembly.

- A pianist preparing for a local music competition; a violinist auditioning for the county youth orchestra; a schoolboy trying for a place in a rock band.

- A young swimmer spending two hours training in the pool every morning before school, hoping to be chosen for the water polo squad; a teenager dedicating every spare moment after school and at weekends, preparing to try out for the Football Academy at a major FA club.

- A young ballet dancer conquering painful feet and sore ankles to dance in her 'toe shoes'; a young performer going from audition to audition, hoping to fulfil his dream of dancing in the chorus of a stage musical.

All of these young people will experience failure, over and over again, from the day-to-day failures in their lessons, coaching sessions and practice (as they tackle and practise more and more complex skills, and face constant correction) to the larger disappointments of failing to make the team, achieving a lower score than they had hoped in a graded music examination, failing to gain a place in the high-profile drama school they had longed to attend.

They are in the process of conquering their fear of failure, of dealing with their nervousness and insecurities, of rising to the challenge. They are making mistakes, but coming back to try again and again. The confidence, resilience and application which come from this kind of long-term commitment to skills development can transform the way in which young people grapple with whatever life holds in store.

Issues for schools

Participation in the creative arts and sport provides a whole range of important benefits for pupils. These can be categorised in two ways:

- **Based on their own intrinsic value:** *the arts and sport provide a different dimension, one which accesses different areas of the brain itself and involves a range of highly developed skills and sensitivities. These are important in their own right, and deserve to be a significant part of every child's education.*

- **Based on their effects on other areas of development:** *involvement in the visual arts, music, dance, drama/theatre and sport has a significant effect on a range of cognitive, affective and creative skills, including social skills, communication, confidence and teamwork.*

Sustained involvement (at whatever level) can provide opportunities for children who are not as able academically to develop confidence and expertise, and there is evidence that this has a 'knock on' effect on their academic achievement.

For all pupils, commitment to develop an area of talent can make a major contribution to academic achievement and personal success.

Raising staff awareness

The benefits for pupils of being 'arts-involved' or 'sports-involved' are sometimes not clear to staff throughout the school, particularly to those members of staff who have never experienced direct involvement in a talent area themselves. With the pressures that all members of staff have to deal with in terms of targets, assessments and so on, it may even seem that rehearsals, games practices, absences for competitions outside school and so on are a distraction from the 'main business of school'.

Some schools have addressed this in innovative ways. For example, one school has introduced a programme where each member of staff – irrespective of their department – has been given a musical instrument to learn for two terms. Working alongside a pupil who has already been playing for a time (in effect being 'mentored' by that pupil), teachers are enjoying working towards an end of year concert where they will show off their skills by joining with pupils in playing some simple arrangements of popular pieces.

In the process they are discovering at first-hand what it means to learn an instrument 'from scratch': how difficult it is to set aside time for practice and to attend rehearsals, how easy it is to forget how to put a clarinet together if it's left untouched for too long, how challenging – and how satisfying – to finally make 'a good sound' on an instrument, to play in a group and not lose one's place in the music, to master one's 'butterflies' before a public performance. This is a first-rate way to raise staff awareness of the kinds of learning, and the range of personal skills, which can be developed through pupils' involvement in a talent area.

The arts and sport within the school community

The status of a subject within the school community can be hard to define. It's not simply a matter of the level of staff salaries or the size of the departmental budget.

In some schools the arts and sport are high-status activities. Pupils and staff in these areas feel valued, and significant numbers pursue these subjects at examination level. In others, arts and PE departments feel isolated and misunderstood, believing their efforts – many of which take place out of school hours – are unappreciated by other staff, parents and pupils.

Yet there are many relatively simple ways to encourage and recognise talent:

- **Awards and prizes** – it is important not to underestimate the value of these. I still cherish a Certificate of Merit for 'excellent service as a member of the Cherokee [Junior High School] Bands' from my middle school; and a 'Most Improved Player' award from the summer camp where I learned to play the trumpet in the marching band!
- **Regular reports in assemblies on non-academic activities** – many schools have weekly reports, often delivered by pupils, on sporting activities, including both outside events and inter-form competitions.
- **Displays of pupils' achievements** – when parents and visitors enter a school for the first time, they gain an immediate impression of what the school values. A regularly updated display of pupils' artwork, a shield won by the choir at a local music festival, cups won by the school's sports teams . . . all of these make a clear statement to parents, prospective parents, staff and pupils about the value the school places on these achievements.

INSET

- Not every school has the time and resources to have every member of staff learn an instrument (see above). What are some practical strategies you might use in your own school, to help make staff aware of the potential benefits of their pupils' involvement in a talent area?

- What is your school's policy towards academic commitments as opposed to those for art, music, drama, dance and PE/sports? Do the academic subjects always take precedence, e.g. do members of staff withdraw pupils from rehearsals without notice to resit a quiz or examination? Is sufficient time made available for rehearsals and training sessions?

- How far have we come since Plowden? Are art, music and PE regarded as 'frills' in your school? What kinds of subtle messages are we giving to parents and pupils about the status of 'non-academic' subjects in our school? Are parents themselves sometimes to blame for a negative attitude to the arts and sport?

- Are there significant differences between primary and secondary schools in terms of the value placed on participation in the arts and sport? What factors might account for these differences?

- Recognition is an important element in raising the status of the talent areas. How are the talent areas represented in your school in terms of awards and prizes, displays of pupils' work, and other indicators of achievement in 'non-academic' areas?

CHAPTER 4

Redefining success

Introduction: success in school terms

Many studies of giftedness and talent take as their starting point individuals who have been highly successful in an area. In fact it is this fascination with 'genius' or 'talent' – often with prodigies of one sort and another – which was the beginning of the entire field of gifted and talented education.

For example, the important work by Sloboda and Ericsson on the development of Expert Performance (see Chapter 2, '"Academic" gifts and "non-academic" talents') takes as its starting point individuals who have been highly successful in a particular area. They begin with the outstanding individual: the one who has 'made it', in his or her field, with a view to increasing our understanding about how they became outstanding (personal characteristics, hours of practice, parental support, etc.) (Ericsson 1996, p. 8). Although their research does much to deepen our concept of giftedness and talent (highlighting the role of personal effort and perseverance), the research is fundamentally 'driven' by a fascination with elite performance. The unspoken assumption is that our goal is to somehow find yet more elite performers, and enable them to reach their potential.

Yet for those of us working in schools – and especially those responsible for identifying and supporting talented pupils – the issues are slightly different. Elite performers in any field are extremely rare: so rare that Ericsson himself points out:

> The small number of individuals performing at these levels makes it difficult to find subjects who are able and willing to participate in extended interviews and laboratory studies.

> (ibid., p. 8)

We are unlikely to find a Mozart or a Beckham in our particular school; some schools may find it difficult even to find a pupil who is performing at County level in a sport; primary schools with no access to instrumental music tuition will be unlikely to find a musical genius in their midst. Many of the pupils we work with will *not* have developed the task commitment needed for outstanding success; others will be distracted by the 'pull' of other interests, abilities and commitments; still others will go through their entire school careers with their talents unrecognised. (The actor, Colin Firth was described by his school head teacher as 'entirely unremarkable', with no sign at all that he would develop into a professional actor.)

Working as we do, in the 'real world', it is important to re-examine some of our thoughts on talent development, and in particular on what constitutes 'success' in school terms.

'Looking for Mozart': two misconceptions about success in the talent area

Misconception One: If you're not going to be a professional artist, sportsman/woman, actor, musician – preferably an outstanding one – you're not really talented

Our culture's fascination with celebrity permeates our attitudes to talent. We're searching for a person of outstanding talent: a Mozart, Beckham, Dame Judi Dench, Picasso, Elton John, Darcy Bussell...We converse in hushed tones about a former student at our local school who has gone on to do great things. (Highly successful pupils often go on to become part of the folklore at their schools, held up as examples to others. I remember visiting one school where I was proudly shown a drum kit donated by a former pupil who had gone on to perform in a well-known rock group. Interestingly, the pupil had not taken part in any school music during his time there, and no one was allowed to use the kit, which was kept as a kind of 'relic'!) At some level we feel that if a student doesn't go on to play at international level in sport, to exhibit at the Tate, to act in the West End, to play in the London Symphony Orchestra, to dance with the Royal Ballet, to perform on *Top of the Pops*, then they're not truly talented.

Yet, for any number of reasons, many talented youngsters will not go on to professional careers in their area of talent.

> **Competition** is fierce for those hoping to enter certain areas of the arts and the highest levels of sport. Success is relative. A youngster who is outstanding in his school may seem very ordinary once he/she starts to compete in the wider world. The 'big fish' in the 'pond' of your locality may not be successful in gaining a place at a top institution, or a part in a West End show. The young hopefuls taking part in shows such as *Pop Idol* and *Fame Academy* have already had some success as performers; yet only a few will go on to have major careers. Of the hundreds of young men each year who try out for places in the training programmes of Premier League football clubs, only a fraction succeed in gaining a place; and still fewer go on to actually play in the first team.
>
> In classical music the picture is the same: every year hundreds of dedicated young performers go through a highly competitive audition system to earn a place at one of the music conservatoires, nationally: the Royal Academy of Music, Royal College of Music, Guildhall School of Music & Drama, Royal Northern College of

Music, Royal Scottish Academy of Music, Birmingham Conservatoire, etc. All will have achieved Grade 8 with Distinction in their instrument. Each institution will field a full symphony orchestra and several minor orchestras, wind ensembles, chamber music groups, and so on. Many of these youngsters will be hoping for careers as orchestral players. Yet there are only a handful of vacancies each year in the major orchestras. Think of the many thousands of pupils who learn the clarinet each year; then think of the hundreds annually who achieve Distinction at Grade 8. Symphony orchestras only have two or three clarinet players; and once a player joins them, they stay for many years – often until retirement. It simply isn't possible for all those who hope to play, to realise their dreams.

Injury or the development of chronic health problems can mean that a talented individual – however dedicated – never 'makes it', or even manages to earn a living in his or her area of talent. An injury can easily put an end to a sporting career; problems with tendons affect violinists and pianists; singers can develop nodules on the larynx; dancers may injure joints and can develop chronic back and foot ailments. In many cases it is the most dedicated who suffer, since many chronic health problems develop from too many hours of 'purposeful practice'.

Financial circumstances can mean that talent is not developed fully. Parents may not be able to afford to pay (and to transport their son/daughter) to the very best teachers in the area; purchasing a really fine instrument may be out of reach; although scholarship help may be available for a few students, groups such as the National Youth Choir, the National Youth Music Theatre and the National Youth Orchestra all involve a parental contribution to the cost of holiday courses. Later in a career, family pressures may mean that hard choices have to be made. I know an opera singer who had to give up a promising career in his mid-twenties to support his extended family when his father became ill with cancer.

Other career choices – Many highly talented pupils – particularly all-rounders, who may have interests and abilities in a whole range of subjects – will make other career choices, choosing to keep their talent area as a much-loved hobby. It is not at all uncommon to find a high court judge who is a professional calibre pianist, or a stockbroker who is a fine artist.

In fact, the medical profession seems to be unusually heavily populated with musicians. I remember joining a high-level amateur orchestra in a large city, some years ago. When I turned up for the first rehearsal I found that doctors and surgeons made up a disproportionate number of the players, including half of the clarinet section. In fact one of the first questions I was asked was, 'Are you a medic?' The same was true of a chamber choir in the same city: three of the seven tenors were doctors, two of them surgeons!

Are these highly skilled musicians 'failures', just because they've chosen to make their living in a different field?

Ian runs a successful small business, which he took over from his father some years ago. In his teens he thought very seriously about pursuing a career in theatre design or in arts administration, but in the end – as the only son – he opted to help his father in the family business. Although not strictly a 'professional', he has had a passionate involvement in theatre for most of his life.

As a child he played one of the 'little princes' in Shakespeare's *Richard III* at the local Theatre Royal. This sparked a keen interest in the theatre, and especially in stage design. At the age of 18 (when he was considering career choices) he was offered a trainee arts management position with a major repertory company some distance from his home. Undecided about career directions, he was torn between stage design, commercial art, and arts administration. With no tradition of careers in the arts within his family, when it came to it he felt uncomfortable about plunging into the world of professional theatre, far away from the small Midlands town where he had grown up.

Although he still has some regrets about turning down the opportunity to work in the arts as a profession, he spends all his free time working in and for the theatre. He still runs the family business, working long hours; but is also Theatre Manager for a major regional amateur theatre company, where he regularly designs productions.

Is Ian a failure in terms of developing and using his talents?

Misconception Two: If your talent doesn't show itself early, it never will

This view arises from our obsession with precocious development. If playing a violin concerto is impressive, playing the same concerto while aged only 12 is even *more* impressive.

Prodigies such as the clarinetist Julian Bliss play the same repertoire as their older counterparts; yet there is a unique fascination in seeing one so young playing music so difficult (see Chapter 5, 'Early developers and prodigies').

Parental influence

From this it is tempting to jump to the conclusion that 'real talent' will show itself at an early age. In fact this kind of precocious development is almost invariably associated with the influence of a highly involved parent. In the case of Julian Bliss, his mother spent hours each day supervising his clarinet practice. With Mozart it was his father, Leopold, who trained Wolfgang and his sister Nannerl to perform before the courts of Europe.

Without this early influence and focus (which presupposes a 'musical family', or a 'sporting family', or an 'artistic family') talent may not 'show early'. My first bassoon pupil was an 11-year-old boy from an 'ordinary' family. He was attracted to the bassoon when I demonstrated it for a group of youngsters who had signed up to learn more mainstream instruments such as the clarinet. Although his fingers wouldn't quite reach the keys, and the school instrument was old, of poor quality and battered from years of use, he 'took to it' and went on to play professionally and teach for a Music Service. His talent certainly didn't 'show early' – but, once discovered, it changed the course of his life.

An early start?

Connected with this preoccupation with prodigies is the view that really talented pupils need to specialise in their talent area from a very young age: that if they haven't made an early start, they will never make it to the highest levels.

While an early start is essential in some areas such as gymnastics, swimming, tennis and classical ballet, in others it is either not appropriate or just not possible. Talented tuba players, electric guitarists and competitive motorcyclists will not emerge until later in their school careers.

In sport, there is a clear time line of physical development, with young people beginning to reach peak performance after the ages of 17 (for girls) and 18 (for boys). Yet there are many areas where physical maturity has to reach a certain level before real talent will show. Examples of this are weightlifting, boxing and competitive rowing. Many experts in the field of sports development currently feel that early, intense specialisation is not a good idea: that in the case of most sports, pupils should receive a broad grounding in general physical skills at primary school level.

It is true that it's much easier to develop physical skills later on, if the groundwork has been laid earlier, during the primary school years. The ballet dancer Sylvie Guillem (the daughter of a gymnastics teacher) originally trained as a gymnast; she didn't begin training as a classical dancer until the age of 11, after discovering her potential during an exchange programme with the Paris Opera Ballet School (see also page 25, Chapter 2).

In music, even the prevailing view that string players need to start young (preferably aged 7–9) is not necessarily true, particularly if a student already reads music comfortably. I recall one 15-year-old pupil – a very capable pianist – sticking his head around the door of the Music Department to say he felt he should learn an orchestral instrument, and that he particularly wanted to learn a stringed instrument, so he could take part in ensembles. I advised him to take up the viola, since they were always in such short supply that he might stand a better chance of getting in to performing groups! He began lessons in Year 10, and by the end of the sixth form he was Grade 7 in Viola – a highly competent level for 'playing for pleasure' at university and beyond.

The American folk artist, Grandma Moses (1860–1961) was a very late developer. She first took up painting in her late seventies, when arthritis made her unable to exercise her lifelong skills in embroidery. From her 'discovery' in 1938 until her death in 1961, she became one of the best-known figures in American art. She had not had any early training in painting: although, again, she was transferring artistic skills from another medium (embroidery), which she had learned earlier in life. (In fact many of her paintings have the 'feel' of an embroidered tapestry.)

Issues for schools

One reason for examining our own preconceptions about the nature of success in the talent area, is the profound effect these preconceptions can have on our pupils' development.

Labelling theory: self-fulfilling prophecies

Several years ago an experiment was conducted with a group of primary school pupils and their teachers. The teachers were told that certain pupils were likely to be showing signs of a spurt in intellectual growth and development in the coming academic year. In fact these pupils had been selected completely at random. At the end of the year the pupils labelled as 'bloomers' had gained an average of 12 IQ points, compared to a gain of 8 points for the unlabelled group. (To read more about this famous experiment (also known as the 'Oak School experiment'), see Rosenthal and Jacobson 1968.)

The latent expectations of their teachers led them to treat the pupils differently. The subtle differences in the ways they worked with those who were expected to do well, meant that the pupils actually did do well.

Although the 'Pygmalion effect' was initially observed in academic subjects, it also has a role to play in the talent domain. The NFER Report Arts Education in Secondary Schools: Effects and Effectiveness (Harland et al. 2000) found that some arts subjects (particularly music) were perceived by secondary school pupils as 'elitist'. If we haven't clarified our own thoughts about the nature of talent and its development, it is easy to inadvertently divide pupils into 'sheep and goats'. For example, a secondary school teacher – by giving an especially warm welcome to those students who have already begun instrumental lessons in primary school – may unconsciously be sending a message to the others that music 'is not for them'.

INSET

Who is more successful – the singer who makes it to the chorus of London shows, but never proceeds to a leading role, or a baritone who is Manager of a large Building Society branch and spends all his spare time singing solos with operatic societies and choral societies throughout his local area (a major city in the Midlands)?

What are some of our own preconceptions about the nature of talent? Is it innate, or can it be developed over time? Is there an age at which it's too late to identify and develop a talent? Is this the same for all talent areas, or are there some where an early start really is essential?

What kind of expectations do we have for our pupils? Do we see them all as potentially talented?

Redefining success

Once we abandon the 'looking for Mozart' approach, defining success in school terms becomes a less daunting task.

We in schools are not in the business of identifying prodigies – we are in the business of nurturing all of our pupils' talents. By offering opportunities and support to all pupils, outstanding individuals will emerge.

I suggest that success in a talent area – what might be termed 'high attainment' – should simply be defined as including pupils who are:

- **Active and committed to the activity while at school:** Those with a *sustained* interest will be able to reap the full benefits of involvement in a talent area, in terms of task commitment, social skills, academic achievement, self-esteem, empathy, and the range of other benefits pupils gain from developing their talents (see Chapter 3, 'The talent area: benefits for pupils').
- **Gaining sufficient skill and motivation to continue being active in a talent area after leaving school:** Pupils with a good grounding in a talent area are much more likely to maintain a connection with that activity in later life, either as a practitioner (a 'hobby for life'), or by having an increased appreciation of an art form or a sport, gained through active participation.

A lifetime practitioner

There are many examples of people whose talents have continued to enrich their lives, long after their initial introduction to the sport or to the art form. Although they did not make it their career, they gained a 'hobby for life'.

- Wartime Prime Minister, Winston Churchill, found great emotional release in painting – a pastime which is also shared by the present Prince of Wales. A more-than-competent artist, Churchill's paintings were widely displayed and appreciated. Although a number of his paintings were eventually sold commercially, he never earned his living primarily through his paintings. Was he a 'failure' as an artist?
- The husband of a friend of mine was a keen rugby player at school. He was also a talented musician, achieving Grade 7 in Piano in his late teens. Now in his fifties, he keeps fit and active playing rugby in a league every Saturday during the season. The family recently purchased a digital piano, and – after a gap of nearly forty years – he is rediscovering the classical piano repertoire he first learned in his childhood and teens. He never reached professional standard in either pursuit. Does this mean that he wasn't a success?

An appreciation gained

Others who devote time to a talent area at school may not pursue it in later life; yet their view of the art form will have been permanently deepened and transformed through the active experience of years of sustained participation. The time spent in developing talents is most emphatically not time wasted.

CASE STUDY

Susanna studied classical dance seriously from the age of three until she was 17. Despite this extended commitment she didn't pursue it as a profession, and jokes modestly that she's not a 'dancer' as she doesn't have any injuries and malformed toes! Now in her mid-twenties, she is extremely fit, eats a healthy diet, is still active in several sports, and remains keenly interested in dance as an art form.

It was Susanna who brought to my attention the quote from Sylvie Guillem (Chapter 2, p. 25) about the amount of time and effort required – in addition to 'talent' – to succeed in dance; and Susanna clearly felt she had benefited greatly from the discipline and commitment involved in her own dance training.

When questioned about why she hadn't gone on to pursue ballet as a career, she said that although passionately interested in dance, it had never been her sole interest. Friends who had gone on to professional careers had focused almost exclusively on dance.

Failing to pursue dance as a career hasn't blighted her life. She was quick to point out that dancing careers are very short and can be plagued by injuries, unhealthy dieting, and so on.

She added an important point: that as a result of her early training she is able to watch ballet with a knowledge and depth of appreciation lacking in those who haven't been so actively involved in the technical aspects of dance. Whereas others might view a performance superficially, Susanna is appreciating it at a completely different level. Her dance training has made her aware of details such as the difficulty of particular movements and steps; and she is also aware of a whole range of issues surrounding different approaches to choreography (something which was entirely new to me, as I've never studied dance). As a result, she feels she is able to understand and enter into the performance in a much more satisfying way.

Note: Susanna contrasted this informed approach to dance performance with her lack of confidence in listening to music. She said she was only able to appreciate a musical performance at a superficial level, since she had never acquired real skills in music. As a result she couldn't hear and understand the detail of what was going on.

Many of us would feel that Susanna has not been a 'failure' by not pursuing her interest and training in classical dance to professional level.

Far from it.

Her experience is a strong argument for redefining our conceptions of success at school level. Her early training has changed her life – and her appreciation of dance as an art form – forever. It has affected her deeply. Hardly 'time wasted', because she didn't 'go on'.

Conclusions

In looking at success in the talent area, we often focus on the end result – the achievement, the medals won, the solos danced or played. If instead we focus on the *process* of talent development, and the many benefits gained by pupils who make a sustained commitment to a talent area, we can begin to develop a clearer view of what it means to succeed. Talent discovery and talent development have a lifelong dimension. Narrow definitions of success can obscure the importance of the 'big picture'.

CHAPTER 5

Early developers and prodigies

Introduction

In the last chapter we discussed how focusing solely on the early developers in a group of pupils could lead to under-identification, especially in the talent area, where important physical skills have to be learned before talent will show. There are many other issues relating to early developers, including the sometimes undue pressure created by the high expectations placed upon youngsters who show early promise.

For the purposes of this chapter, early developers and prodigies are those who show skills in advance of their years. In school terms, this can range from a pupil who simply picks things up more quickly than others (thereby showing 'early promise'), to one who has systematically developed his or her talents outside school, to an unusually high level.

In the first category, I know of a ten-year-old boy who responded so well to a series of three dance workshops at his primary school, that within a year he was a pupil at the Royal Ballet School. He picked things up so quickly that even his classroom teacher – who had had no previous exposure to classical dance – could see that he was 'something special'. Those who have systematically developed their talents outside school might include a girl I know who was already working towards her Grade 7 examination in cello while only in Year 8 (the standard of performance expected for GCSE level in Year 11 is Grade 5). Likewise, youngsters who are 'ahead' in terms of ball-handling skills, or swimming, would be classed as early developers.

A prodigy is simply an early developer who is so advanced that his/her achievements are extraordinary, rather than just exceptional. Take, for example, Yehudi Menuhin (1916–1999), who was the first child violin prodigy to emerge from the United States. By the age of seven he was renowned for his playing of the Mendelssohn violin concerto, and – unlike many prodigies – while still in his teens he was regarded as one of the 'greats' in terms of musical interpretation as well as technical skill. In 1963, he founded the Yehudi Menuhin School in

Cobham, Surrey, to provide specialised training for highly talented young musicians.[1]

All of us working in schools will have met early developers, but few will have worked with prodigies. Yet many of the issues facing the two groups are similar.

Over-generalising about the talent areas ... a dangerous pursuit

Before systematically looking at some of the issues faced by early developers in sport, the performing arts (drama, music and dance) and the visual arts, it is important to note that these are all very different areas. And while they are linked together, in that they all require long-term development of physical skills, the differences between them often outweigh the similarities.

For example, I am often struck by the parallels between the kind of teamwork involved in being a member of a sports team, and in being a member of a musical ensemble; yet it is harder to see the link between these collaborative efforts and some of the visual arts, which tend to focus more on individual endeavour. However in terms of self-expression, music and the visual arts have much more in common. (Perhaps the link there is between composing and the visual arts, both of which require reflection, trial and error and skilful reworking of outcomes.) There is certainly a very real difference between those talent activities which take place in 'real time' – under the pressure of performance, whether a competition or a concert – and those which are predominantly individual and reflective. They require very different temperaments and appeal to a very different range of students.

What *is* true is that it is impossible to generalise about the talent area, as it covers such a wide range of activities. Leaving aside the huge variety of sporting pursuits (from snooker to weightlifting to international football) and looking solely at the visual and performing arts, there are clear contrasts between the various art forms. The NFER Report *Arts Education in Secondary Schools: Effects and Effectiveness* (Harland *et al.* 2000) revealed marked differences between art, dance, drama and music, in both their overall health within the context of schools, and in terms of the effects on pupils. In terms of outcomes, it concludes that

> the use of the term 'the arts' might be unhelpful if it leads to policies which wrongly assume that the learning gains associated with one art form are broadly the same as those of the others.

(p. 1)

---

1   The Menuhin School educates around fifty musically gifted boys and girls, both string players and pianists. Since 1973 it has been designated a Centre of Excellence for the Performing Arts by the DfES. This means that all UK pupils at the school are supported by the DfES Music and Dance Scheme, which helps to fund places at a small number of specialist music and dance schools (nine in all, including Chetham's School of Music, and the Royal Ballet School). Full details of the scheme are available on the DfES website (www.dfes.gov.uk).

Early developers: the curse of precocious development?

Although the word 'prodigy' simply means someone extraordinary – someone whose talents excite admiration and wonder – we tend to reserve the term for people who exhibit this development in childhood, well in advance of the usual age: in other words, with precocious development. As discussed briefly in Chapter 4 ('Redefining success') we as a culture seem to be obsessed with precocious development. Anyone who has been a parent knows how avidly we watch our offspring, noting every milestone of our child's development: his or her first words, first steps and so on. This is one way in which we measure normal development. But it soon becomes clear that some children are reaching these milestones rather sooner than others. So it may be that this very fundamental aspect of the human experience is the foundation of our obsession with early developers.

Success in the adult world

We persist in identifying as 'exceptional' those who show precocious development, while at the same time – almost as an afterthought – we document the fact that few prodigies go on to fulfil their potential in the adult world.

Performance in the adult world is a sticky issue for early developers and prodigies. Many writers define exceptional performance in adult life as 'expanding the frontiers of a particular domain'. Einstein's contribution to physics would be an example of this, as would Beethoven's contribution to the development of the symphony. Yet prodigies seldom, if ever, 'expand the frontiers' of their particular domain. This is something which only happens later on, after they have mastered the domain in the first place. Winner and Martino, in their article 'Giftedness in non-academic domains: the case of the visual arts and music' point this out:

> A prodigy is someone who can easily and rapidly master a domain with expertise. A creator is someone who changes a domain … The skill of being a prodigy is not the same as the skill of being a … creator.
>
> (Winner and Martino 2000, p. 107)

Think of early developers such as Charlotte Church, who became famous for singing the adult repertoire of opera and oratorio. Signed by Sony to a multi-album recording contract at the age of 11, her first album became number one in the UK Classical Charts two years later. Yet leaving aside the important question of whether it is wise in the long term for one so young to develop their voice in this way, it is unlikely that any of her interpretations of famous arias and songs will enter the canon of greatness. That is not to say that Charlotte may not develop into one of the finest singers of our age. But she hasn't done so yet. The fascination was with one so young singing pieces which were so difficult.

The essence of being a prodigy is in reproducing the works and interpretations of others. It is only later that one has 'something to say' in interpreting the song or an operatic role, since it is impossible to express love, hate, lust, rage and fear without experiencing a bit more of life. I recall struggling to explain the context of a love song to one of my students – a lad of 15 – who was working towards a Grade 7 examination in Singing. The chap in the song had fallen madly in love with someone who didn't love him in return. The song lurched from emotion to emotion, first pining for her and begging her to notice him, then in the next moment, hating her. It didn't seem to make much sense to my young singer. Disarmingly, he eventually said, 'But I haven't been in love yet!'[2]

And, of course, there's also the possibility that an early developer may 'burn out' and react against his/her area of talent with the onset of adolescence. (Charlotte Church's interests have now turned to pop music.)

In the case of child actors, the challenge of making the transition to a lifelong career has proven difficult for many, if not most. Sadly, in a number of well-documented cases, this has also been associated with psychological and addiction problems.

Of course, many early developers do go on to have fine careers. This is particularly true in sport and in dance. The tennis player, Boris Becker, made a huge impression at the age of 17, by becoming the youngest male to win Wimbledon. He then went on to play in Wimbledon finals in six of the next seven years, and to win again twice more. The ballet dancer, Carlos Acosta, won a major dance competition – also at the age of 17 – and has had a fine career as Principal Dancer both in Britain and in the United States.

Great expectations: the pressures of 'early promise'

This brings up another issue: the pressure which can result from the label 'precocious' or 'prodigy'. Child actors and musical prodigies are already familiar with the difficulties that can arise when all the fuss has died down, and they have to fulfil their potential in adult life.

However, these kinds of pressures are present to some extent in the lives of many, if not most, early developers. While it is true that many pupils enjoy being seen as precocious, the reality is that many early developers are to a greater or lesser degree subjected to an unremitting pressure of expectations (from parents, teachers, pupils and, most of all, from themselves).[3]

The right to fail

In terms of achievement, early recognition as 'something special' in whatever the area (academic or non-academic) can increase self-consciousness to the point where a

---

2   This mismatch of emotional maturity with repertoire is very common. I had a similar difficulty with another 15-year-old who did not immediately understand a song called 'The Lads in their hundreds', which dealt with young men going off to the First World War, some of them never to return. He was also an 'early developer', whose voice had shifted comfortably (without a 'break') to tenor, and was working on much higher grades, technically, than most singers his age.

3   When this is coupled with the dislike of their peers, sparked by jealousy, it can have a devastating effect on pupils' development and self-esteem.

youngster is frightened to try anything difficult in case they do not excel. By being labelled as outstanding, they can lose the right to fail, and to learn from those failures. And since the talent area is linked so strongly to training and practice, they will also fail to develop the skills they need to make the most of their abilities.

It is not necessary to be a prodigy in order to suffer from this kind of pressure. It can happen to children from supportive backgrounds in supportive schools. These are the sorts of pupils we might expect to run across in every year group: those who might conceivably go on to make a career in a talent area.

Avoiding the difficult bits

CASE STUDY

I know in my own case I was spotted as a talented bassoon player in middle school. Once the word was out, I became increasingly uncomfortable about practising any of the bits I couldn't play! Eventually, even in practice at home I avoided anything I couldn't master on the first or second try; and since this didn't include any sort of difficult scales or technical exercises, any high notes (where I didn't know the fingerings very well) or any particularly fast passages, eventually I was no longer the favoured young bassoonist. Soon, a younger pupil – who, incidentally, came from a musical family – took up the bassoon and did practice 'the difficult bits', in time overtaking me. By the time we reached the senior school, young Alex had become first chair bassoon in the Senior Wind Ensemble, with me languishing at third bassoon, still avoiding learning those awkward scales. It was only much later on, as a young adult, when I finally learned how to practise effectively: by focusing almost solely on the difficult bits! But by then it was too late for a career as an orchestral bassoon player.

Note: One advantage of having a musical family is that they understand about the need to practise the difficult bits, whereas my family unwittingly added to the pressure, by expecting practice sessions to sound wonderful. My bassoon was known at home as the 'belching bedpost', which made me very self-conscious about practising at home at all!

Punishment by rewards

Alfie Kohn (1999), in his book *Punished by Rewards*, argues that rewards and recognition can in fact have a negative effect on development.[4] Since many of the talent areas involve competitions and awards of one sort and another, his views are particularly apt.

---

4   Although Kohn's views have been challenged, those of us who have worked in schools will all know of pupils who 'went off' after receiving a reward. Somehow their attitude changed, and not for the better.

CASE STUDY

I know of a young singer who had a reputation for not working hard in her voice lessons. She would turn up week after week, having done no practice at all. Since she never practised her technique, she never improved. And if asked to memorise a piece, she somehow never got around to it. Often she left the music in her locker or at home. The result was total frustration for the teacher, who would work hard in the lesson, see real improvement, and deliver encouragement by the bucketload, only to find that at the next lesson they were back to square one. Finally the teacher decided to have a heart to heart talk. Once the girl's defensive approach had lessened a bit, the real reasons for her lack of motivation began to emerge.

It seems that she had won a school talent competition in middle school. Without any training, she had sung so well that not only had her classmates praised her, but her music teacher had said enthusiastically that she had so much talent in singing that she must have voice lessons. Her parents had duly arranged for her to begin the lessons in the next term. The girl responded enthusiastically, and at first made good progress. Then came the time for the talent competition the next year. She now had a reputation to live up to: friends, parents and teachers alike expected her to be even better this year – to win the top prize.

Instead, she started to shake with nerves. All of her vocal technique – which was still in the early stages of development, and not yet well-established – went out the window. She failed to live up to (her own and others') expectations, and worried that she could no longer find the 'natural voice' which had seemed so effortless last year, when there been no pressure to succeed.

To protect herself from further failure, she became offhand about her lessons, and soon developed a veneer of not caring about her singing. Nothing could be further from the truth. She cared very deeply – in fact, too deeply. Basking in the attention gained at that first talent competition (when she had won so effortlessly), she had allowed herself to 'dream dreams' and imagine herself going on to sing professionally. The pressure of expectations had actually inhibited the development of her initial promise.

Early development in sport

Varying rates of physical development mean that there will always be early developers in sport. It is well known that boys born at certain times of the year are disproportionately represented in school sports teams, simply by virtue of their advanced physical development. This pattern of success, once established, continues, and also holds true for professional sports teams. Those who are larger and stronger have a natural advantage in environments where sports teams are generally defined by the age ranges of year groups (which, incidentally, is an argument for forming at least some extramural teams by ability and physical maturity rather than by age).

Paradoxically, this age advantage does not seem to apply so much in the case of girls – possibly because girls' sports are less dependent on size and strength. It also seems that boys born at the 'wrong' time of year suffer more in terms of confidence and self-esteem (which at this age are so tied up with size and strength) from this age-related discrimination in sport. As a result, many from an early age decide they are not 'sporty'.

As for prodigies, they certainly do exist in the sporting field. One only has to think of the attention given to Michael Owen when he made the England football squad at a tender age. However, this kind of fame lasts only briefly: within just a few years another player, Wayne Rooney, broke Owen's record by being the youngest player ever to score in an international match for England. The eternal problem for *any* prodigy is the unavoidable fact that the *next* prodigy is already at work, training and practising to dethrone the current media favourite.

The issue of whether or not to positively *encourage* early development through early training in specific sports has been a matter of some discussion and dispute over the years. The current view shared by many coaches and experts in the field is that there are two models which are appropriate for different types of sports.

- **Early Specialisation Model:** In some sports (e.g. gymnastics, rhythmic gymnastics, figure-skating, diving, swimming and tennis) training needs to start early. Training in these areas will be intensive and time consuming. Pupils involved in early specialisation sports may well be spending three or more hours a day during the school week, perfecting their skills. (The same is true in classical ballet, where the hours of intensive training begin during the primary school years.)

- **Late Specialisation Model:** This model applies to the vast majority of sports including athletics, rowing and all team sports. Research has suggested that specialisation before the age of ten is not appropriate for these sports, since it contributes to early burn-out and high drop-out rates. In the Late Specialisation Model (favoured by the UK's Institute of Youth Sport), boys and girls aged six to ten take part in a **FUNdamentals** stage, which is designed to develop speed, power and endurance, coupled with learning correct techniques in the basics of many sports, e.g. throwing, running, and jumping. The aim is to produce youngsters who can specialise later on: when their physical development is more advanced, and better choices can be made as to which sports are most appropriate for a particular individual.

Rather than encourage precocious development when it is not needed, the Late Specialisation Model is a conscious attempt to slow things down until pupils are more mature – a model which might well be imitated by some of the other talent areas.

Early developers in the visual arts

Most of us learn very early in life to handle pen, pencil and paper. As a result art is one of the most accessible and successful arts subjects in school terms, e.g. in numbers of pupils taking the subject at GCSE. According to the NFER Report on *Arts Education in Secondary Schools: Effects and Effectiveness*, art was:

The strongest and most robust of the art forms.

(Harland *et al.* 2000, p. 6)

Since expressing oneself through art is so accessible, it is not unusual to find early developers in art. Its inclusivity means that there is to some extent a more 'level playing field' in art (and to some extent in PE).[5] At primary school level these tend to be pupils who master representational art particularly easily, e.g. by being able to reproduce a drawing or copy an intricate design. At secondary school, it may be those who produce the most striking work, who are identified as 'advanced' in art. This can make it difficult to identify outstanding talent, since a child drawing in an unconventional way at primary school (where realism is more the aim) might be criticised by the teacher: those we think of as 'early developers' in primary school may turn out to have very little flair, once they reach secondary school.

Likewise, those with a flair for more representational or 'applied' art may feel undervalued in secondary schools.

CASE STUDY

Sue is a highly successful graphic artist who felt undervalued in her (academically selective) secondary school, where the Head of Art focused heavily on fine art. In fact Sue was actively discouraged from doing A-level art at her school, and was told outright that she had 'no talent' for art. In the end she transferred to a college which specialised in commercial art, and went on to a successful career in computer graphics, specialising in television work. She currently teaches at a local college, passing on her skills in commercial art.

Although this is clearly an extreme case, there are lessons to be learned in terms of teachers' (and schools') expectations in the creative arts, where subjective judgements can cloud our assessment of a pupil's talents.

While in music, prodigies are relatively commonplace, in art these are very rare. This may be because we value different things in the other arts. In drama, dance and music, prodigies are admired primarily for *reproducing other people's work*. (Prodigies in musical composition are exceedingly rare. And there are very few ten-year-old playwrights and choreographers![6]) What we are admiring – and which

---

5 This is not to undervalue the importance of fine teaching, which can liberate pupils' talents in all of the talent areas.

6 This is not to say that youngsters can not show early *promise* as a composer, choreographer or playwright, particularly if given the opportunity to do so by their teachers. However, very few will possess the range of skills needed to achieve a professional standard in these fields. This is because they need to master so many other skills first. In composition, for example, a child may well show imagination, and a natural sense of structure and style, yet lack the skills to write effectively for the instruments involved. Similarly, in dance an outstanding choreographer needs not only a thorough knowledge of the moves available, but the experience of a range of styles, and a deep appreciation of what is possible (and impossible) for the dancers he or she is working with.

makes them so exceptional – is their ability to perform other people's work to a high standard at an early age, not to create work of their own. By contrast, in art it is originality that we value, coupled with the capacity to capture a particular style.

Another reason for the relative rarity of prodigies in art is the fact that it is so accessible. The other arts are less so. The parents of musical prodigies will have made a major commitment to helping their child to acquire specialist training, purchasing an instrument, and encouraging regular practice. Child actors often have parents who are keenly involved in the theatre. By the middle of primary school, the parents of many young dancers will already have invested considerable time and energy in supporting their child's dance training. By getting a 'head start' they are on the way to showing exceptional 'early promise'. (If pupils haven't been exposed to a particular set of skills, they are unlikely to show exceptional ability in that area.) In art – where from nursery onwards all pupils will have had the opportunity to practise skills in drawing and painting – the contrast between those with keen parents and those without will be less noticeable.

Issues for schools: early developers

- Pupils whose development is in advance of their peers need encouragement and recognition; but this needs to be done without undue pressure and attention. Like all pupils, they need 'permission' to grow and develop without fear of failure.

- Schools need to be aware that in the case of Early Specialisation Model sports, classical dance and some types of music performance, pupils of primary school age may already be under significant pressure in terms of time and training and expectations.

- Be aware that outstanding performance in childhood is no guarantee of success in later life. Early developers need to develop the same kinds of social skills and task commitment that all pupils need in order to make the most of their abilities in the adult world.

- Pupils who have achieved early success may attract negative attention from their less talented peers. They may need help in coming to terms with this, or their self-esteem and social development may suffer.

- The gap between technical proficiency and emotional and physical maturity may mean that some early developers are placed in situations which are inappropriate, e.g. I had a bassoon pupil once who gained a place in a youth orchestra at the age of 13; as the youngest wind player in the orchestra, he was initially very pleased and proud of his achievement. However, since the average age of the other players was 'across the great divide' of puberty, he felt isolated socially, and unhappy. In the end he dropped out of the orchestra, rejoining it – very successfully – two years later.

- Early developers in any area may have achieved their early success through the over-involvement of a parent in the child's progress. This means that when adolescence comes, they may react negatively to their area of talent. Some will decide they aren't really interested in the sport or art form, and move on to something else. Others will feel this for a time, but then return to the fold. Schools need to be sensitive to this process, and to be understanding in their dealings with concerned parents.

INSET

- Which of your current pupils show signs of precocious development in a talent area?
- Has this been beneficial to them in social terms? (This can vary, depending on the talent area and the ethos of the school, e.g. early developers in art or sport may be more popular than those who show exceptional promise in classical dance.)
- Do you know of any pupils who have been 'punished by rewards'? (See above, pp. 50–1.) How can we acknowledge pupils' achievements without placing them under undue pressure to succeed?
- In what ways can the school help to support pupils who are undergoing long hours of intensive training in a talent area, often while still at primary school?

Late developers and all-rounders

Late developers

Late developers (or, as they are sometimes called, 'late bloomers') have their own set of issues. Since encouragement and recognition tend to go to the early developers, those whose talents are not discovered and developed until later than usual may be at a distinct disadvantage. Late developers are often 'under-identified' and – partly as a result of low expectations (their own and others') – they often underachieve. Particularly in economically and socially deprived areas, pupils are less likely to have had an early start; they may therefore compare unfavourably with pupils from social groups where talent development is regarded as an essential part of every child's upbringing. (This is not always an advantage. For some pupils from well-to-do homes, the endless round of piano lessons, judo classes, tennis camps and the like can make them feel as if they are being force-fed with 'polite accomplishments'.)

Of course, in many of the talent areas (especially in sport, in classical dance and in some areas of music performance) the 'clock is ticking' in terms of physical development. Those who do not have an early start, or whose development is delayed by any number of factors, can find that avenues are closed to them.

When Joan Freeman visited the homes of some youngsters she was studying in Walsall several years ago, she found that 'artistic' pupils came from 'arty' homes, musical pupils from 'musical homes', and so on. This is not surprising, since parents who are passionate about a talent area (whether it be music, art, sport, drama, or dance) can hardly wait to share it with their offspring.

CASE STUDY

In 'musical families' early discussions take place around what instrument the child will play. One couple I know were seriously concerned when their baby daughter had a bad fall while learning to walk. She had to have stitches on her top lip, and the mother (a fine clarinetist) was concerned that it might affect the child's embouchure for playing the clarinet. (The father was a string player, so fortunately there was a back-up plan!)

The same is, of course, true for 'sporting' families. It is not long before the children of keen skiers are tumbling their way down the slopes. And many a young actor or actress has appeared in a play when well under the age of ten!

While it is good to know that families are successfully passing on their skills and knowledge to their children, one cannot help but wonder about pupils from more 'ordinary' homes. Would some of them have shown real talent if they had had the benefit of growing up in an environment where, from an early age, participation in a talent area was the norm?

Late starters

It is important to distinguish between **late starters** and **late developers**. A **late starter** is someone who began an activity later in their school career, but then took to it like the proverbial duck to water. In some cases this is because they have transferable skills – developed in other talent areas – which help them to 'catch up' with those who started the activity at 'the usual age'. We usually think of ballet as an area where an early start is essential. Yet sometimes late starters can not only go on to have a successful career: they also bring new elements to their conception of dance.

CASE STUDY

The ballet dancer, Carlos Acosta (one of the eleven children of a truck driver) excelled at break dancing and dreamt of a career as a footballer. After his mother's death, his father became concerned that the boy might be drifting towards getting into trouble with the law. He insisted that Carlos attend a local ballet school with some neighbours' children. Carlos admits that at that time he hated ballet!

After a school visit to see the National Ballet of Cuba, he suddenly had a vision of himself as a dancer, and threw himself into his work. At the age of 17, he took the world by storm, winning a major international competition in Italy; from there he went on to be Principal Dancer at the Royal Ballet in London.

Like Sylvie Guillem (see Chapter 2, p. 25), whose early background in gymnastics had a significant effect on her style of dance, Carlos's work – particularly with young people in his native Cuba – expands the usual range of ballet to include many elements of the popular dance forms he delighted in as a young boy.

Late starters can also achieve success in **sport**. Often the late start is triggered by an interest in a sport which is not on offer until secondary school, or even later. For example, several of the rowers in a recent Oxford versus Cambridge boat race had not sampled the sport until they arrived at university. Although a late start in sport may preclude a professional career, in school terms it is still in time to enjoy many of the benefits of participation in the talent area, both at school and in later life.

CASE STUDY

I went through the local primary and secondary school with Martin, a distinctly non-sporty 'boffin', who seemed to despise PE, and sport of all types. (Perhaps he was one of those with a birthday in the 'wrong' time of the year...) When he entered the senior high school aged 15, he decided that he was missing out on an aspect of his development, and volunteered for the (open-access) school wrestling team. Wrestling competitions are determined by weight, rather than by chronological age, so he found he was matched against others who were also relatively short, and lightly built. Although he never became a star, he did become a useful member of the team, and took part successfully in a number of competitions. He clearly gained much from the experience, and in the school yearbook he is proudly pictured in the wrestling team photo.

In the **visual arts**, probably the most spectacularly late starter was the folk artist Grandma Moses (also mentioned in Chapter 4, 'Redefining success'). Like Carlos Acosta, she had some transferable skills.

CASE STUDY

Grandma Moses began painting in her late seventies, when arthritic fingers precluded the embroidery work she had excelled in for most of her life. By the time of her death (aged 101) in 1961, she was known throughout the world for the beautiful simplicity and rich colours of her 'primitivist school' paintings. In fact she was something of a sensation. (It's tempting to think that some of her originality derived directly from reinterpreting some of the techniques of traditional embroidery, in her painting.)

Issues for schools: late starters
In school terms, this is an important issue, particularly for secondary schools:

■ *Don't prejudge pupils' potential in the talent areas. This is particularly important at the transition from primary to secondary school. Youngsters who come in to secondary school – like Martin, 'turned off' on sport – may suddenly find a new sport on offer which interests them. Pupils who struggled with pen and paper may find that using ICT to create digital art liberates their imagination.*

CASE STUDY

Thomas struggled to learn the trumpet in primary school. His elder brother was an exceptionally good trumpet player, and the younger son may have felt intimidated by this. Whatever the reason (or set of reasons) he gave up his lessons in primary school after a year. Yet when introduced to the tuba at secondary school, he suddenly 'took off', and has gone on to a career in one of the Forces Bands.

In fact, both boys grew up to be full-time professional musicians. They were not from a 'musical home', and attended a tiny, rural primary school in a remote area: a real success story for the schools involved, and for the parents, who supported the boys' activities to the full.

- *Don't prejudge pupils who have already 'had a go' at a talent area (e.g. instrumental music lessons) in primary school but who didn't continue. Some teachers are reluctant to give valuable instrumental lesson time to youngsters who have already had a go and failed to progress. This can be a mistake: their previous experience will give them a head start on general aspects of learning an instrument, such as reading music; and it may simply be that the instrument they tried before was not the one for them.*

CASE STUDY

I recall a bassoon student (aged 14) who had already tried to play the oboe in primary school and the clarinet in Year 8. He didn't seem a particularly promising candidate, but I was looking for someone to learn to play the school bassoon, and he volunteered. He took to the instrument immediately, and regularly wore out reeds from practising! Within two years he was playing in the County Youth Orchestra, had taught himself to play the piano to Grade 6 standard, and was thinking of applying to the Royal Academy of Music as a bassoonist.

- *Ensure a fair and consistent approach to late starters. With limited resources – and the common preconception that early development is best – there is a temptation to focus on younger pupils. I know of cases where pupils 'put their names down' for instrumental lessons at the beginning of secondary school, but never made it to the top of the list. The next year, incoming 11-year-olds were given places, and the older pupils passed over. These discouraging experiences can have a heavy impact on a pupil's self-esteem. This is not to say that older pupils should always be given preference. The essential ingredient is motivation: if the activity is 'right' for them, a highly-motivated older youngster can soon make up lost ground.*

INSET

- Does your department or faculty have a policy on late starters? What practical issues are involved, e.g. when limited places are available?
- What is your own experience of pupils who took up an activity later than the norm? How did it benefit them? What problems were encountered?
- Is access to clubs in the talent areas restricted by age range? There is some evidence that clubs which cross year boundaries have real advantages, allowing late starters (and early developers, as well) to interact with those who are 'at their level', in a less formal environment.

Late development: some causes and consequences

True late developers are a slightly different case. Unlike late starters, they will have been exposed to the activity, but without showing early promise. In fact they may struggle at first, but keep plodding along. It is only later on that their exceptional talents show.

Listed below are some of the causes of late development:

- **Illness or physical disability:** This can delay and/or impede development, yet talent may still be there in abundance.

> **CASE STUDY**
>
> The lyricist and writer, Richard Stilgoe and his wife Annabel are co-founders of the **Orpheus Trust**, which supports young disabled people in the fields of music and drama. Through a series of courses and apprenticeships, participants are able to develop their skills in the performing arts. This unique experiment allows disabled young people to perform in a first-class theatre, and to develop a range of skills – not only musical, but also life skills. They have performed in an astounding range of venues, including the Royal Opera House, Glastonbury and the Queen Elizabeth Hall. The young people (several of whom are in wheelchairs and suffer multiple disabilities), express themselves musically with impressive confidence, warmth and poignancy.

- **Later physical maturity:** This is particularly noticeable in boys. A late growth spurt can suddenly aid access to sports (such as basketball) where physical size is an advantage. Thus encouraged, a mediocre player may find the motivation to devote himself wholeheartedly to developing his other playing skills and emerge as a potential 'star'. This is also true of singers – both boys and girls – who are often in their mid to late teens before discovering their 'voice'.

- **Pupils from 'ordinary' families:** Youngsters who lack a strong home background in their talent domain will be starting from a much lower base. As a result they may find it a slow business to develop their potential in that area. In general, musicians who become exceptional performers are those who have had the benefit of musically stimulating home environments as children. A child who grows up in a home where the arts and/or sport are valued, will have gained a whole range of skills and knowledge. At a very young age they will already be wondering which instrument(s) they will play, or what sport they will concentrate on. If the parents are actively involved in a talent area (either as professionals or as amateurs) they will have attended rehearsals, games and practice sessions. They will have seen older brothers and sisters progress through the ranks of the local swimming club, or audition to gain a place in the back row of the second violins in the local (or even National) Youth Orchestra. They may even have taken part in a performance, e.g. see Ian's case study in

Chapter 4 (p. 40). They 'know the ropes'. (For a fuller discussion of this, see Davidson *et al.* 1996 and Sloboda and Howe 1992.) For those who haven't been introduced to a talent area at home, there may be a steep 'learning curve' while they pick up the basic skills necessary to excel.[1]

CASE STUDY

James and Akash (both aged ten) began flute lessons at school. James was from a 'musical' home, and had already had two years of piano lessons. Music-reading was no problem for him, and he had been to concerts and heard recordings of some fine flute players. His elder sister was working towards her Grade 5 Clarinet examination, so he knew what it meant to practise regularly, and the importance of 'doing his scales'. Having taken a Grade 1 Piano examination, he also knew about the aural tests, sight-reading and so on, which are important elements of these examinations. James's mother insisted that he have flute lessons: there was a flute at home which had belonged to her when she was at school; and at James's primary school the first term's lessons were free of charge.

Akash chose the flute because he thought it would be the kind of flute he was familiar with from gatherings in his local Asian community; and was surprised to find that this kind of flute was held sideways! No one in his family or extended family had ever learned an instrument at school or at home. He had never read music, played another instrument or sung in a choir. Yet he loved to play the flute, and practised diligently. Soon he was the most reliable at getting a good sound out of the flute, in his group lesson. At a Parents' Evening his mother told how he carried the flute with him all over the house, playing constantly. She and his father were thrilled to see how much he enjoyed playing, and at the end of the first two terms of lessons, they bought him his own instrument to replace the flute he had on loan from the school.

The case of the second boy is typical of many pupils from different ethnic backgrounds. Asian music is very different from the Western classical music that is the mainstay of most instrumental music lessons in schools. Learning an instrument is not easy: it involves struggling to learn how to put the instrument together without breaking it (no mean feat!), how to make a good sound, how to get 'across the break' in fingering, etc. But Akash had the additional challenges of learning to read music, and beginning to develop an 'ear' for what makes a good sound on this type of flute.

---

1 As part of the UK Government's 'Wider Opportunities' initiative (to provide greater access to instrumental tuition for primary school children), a pilot study in Kirklees has shown that when socially disadvantaged primary school pupils are given the kind of background in general musicianship that pupils from 'musical homes' experience, coupled with the opportunity to try a range of instruments in 'taster' sessions, there is a much higher take up of instrumental lessons (and, interestingly, a higher take up of less 'popular' instruments such as violin and cello). By mimicking a musically rich home environment, pupils are given a head start in successfully learning an instrument.

At the end of the year, both boys were entered for a Grade 1 examination in Flute. James achieved a Merit; Akash, a low pass. But by now Akash was ' hooked' on playing the flute. He was a regular attendee at Junior Band rehearsals and a Flute Ensemble at his school. In time he joined other musical groups, at the County Music Service. He didn't give up, and by Grade 5 he was the one achieving a Merit.

James, by the way, soon became bored with the flute, and gave up the lessons after his Grade 1 examination. He preferred to play the piano, and didn't really have the time to learn another instrument. His mother had insisted that he have the flute lessons, even though he wasn't particularly interested. (Sadly, this is a typical story, too!)

■ **Poor initial tuition/coaching:** The development of the physical skills inherent in talent areas is dependent on good coaching and continued intervention and modelling. Therefore good teaching/coaching at beginner level is vital if talent is to show early. Experts in sport and physical education strongly recommend that experienced coaches teach throughout the ability range, so that beginners can have the benefit of their expertise. The particular importance of the coach or teacher in the talent realm means that a change of teacher can make a huge difference. With good tuition a pupil whose poor technique was holding them back, can suddenly blossom.

CASE STUDY

Jane began piano lessons at the age of eight, with a local piano teacher who lived near her home. The teacher was a competent pianist, but had not played at a high level, and had no formal qualifications in teaching. She was at home, with a young family; and piano teaching seemed a convenient and flexible way to earn some extra cash. Jane's mother had never learned an instrument, and knew nothing about choosing a suitable teacher. Jane's teacher lived conveniently nearby, and some of Jane's friends already went to her for lessons.

Jane enjoyed playing the piano, and spent long hours practising. However, her teacher lacked the necessary skills and knowledge to establish a good basic technique. As a result, Jane's playing was nothing special, and even her parents thought of her as 'a plodder'. Many years later – while at university – Jane decided to invest in some lessons with a highly regarded teacher, who had played professionally and had trained at the Royal College of Music. Within two months her playing was transformed! She had lacked the technique necessary to express herself through her chosen instrument. A change of teacher made all the difference, at last unlocking her musical talent.

■ **Some people are just slower to develop the skills and attributes needed, despite plenty of motivation and family support:** An example of this type of late development was the famous actor, Sir John Gielgud. He came from a highly 'theatrical' family, with a long tradition of producing actors and actresses of distinction. By his late teens, he was still unsure whether he wanted to be an actor, or go into stage design. More importantly (particularly in the theatrical climate of the day, where 'classical training' in voice and movement was an important prerequisite for success), he was clumsy and, by his own admission, 'moved very badly':

at first, what frightened me was that I moved very badly. I have always hated sport, played no games, I couldn't swim, I couldn't really do anything. Later, when I learned to drive a car, I even had to give that up because I was so clumsy.

(Quoted in Morley 2001, p. 24)

In his first professional stage performance (aged 17), as the Herald in *Henry V*:

John had said his one line, 'Here is the number of the slaughtered French,' so badly that for the rest of the season he was not given another word to speak. So unpromising did he seem to the 'real' actors in the company that many of them…took the trouble to come over and tell him that despite his theatrical heritage he would be well advised to give up any thought of the professional stage.

(*ibid.*, p. 31)

And, interestingly enough, in light of what we've already seen about the importance of task commitment:

Curiously, it was this opposition that finally tipped the balance and made him now, for the first time, determined to be an actor.

(*ibid.*, p. 32)

Some consequences of late development

Many late developers will find that career opportunities – particularly in 'early specialisation' sports such as tennis, gymnastics and swimming, and in classical dance – may be out of their reach. Careers in sport and dance begin early and coincide with peaks in physical condition, agility, etc. Significantly late developers may find that some doors are closed to them. However, the skills gained and the ability to express themselves through their talents are immensely valuable and life-enriching.

Issues for schools: late developers

- *Avoid making early judgements as to the degree of talent a pupil might possess, since achievement may be masked by lack of opportunity, home background, etc.*
- *Don't go overboard the other way, either, by actively disadvantaging pupils from 'sporty' or 'artistic' homes. They deserve support, too.*
- *Try to create an atmosphere where early developers and late developers alike feel valued.*
- *Avoid pressuring late developers to take examinations or enter competitions too early.*

They can become discouraged, and give up. Let them take their time: it's better to have a successful and positive experience later on, rather than a mediocre experience early on.
- *Encourage teachers who specialise in art, music, drama and PE to teach throughout the age range, so that younger pupils can benefit from fine teaching at the 'beginner' stage.*
- *Remember that disabled young people may have exceptional talents, and ensure that they are considered for inclusion on the register of gifted and talented pupils at your school.*

INSET

- Are there opportunities for younger pupils in your school to work with the most capable and inspiring coaches and teachers? Or are their timetables taken up primarily with senior groups?
- What are some of the ways in which disabled youngsters might be enabled to express themselves through the arts and sport? (Technology can help pupils – particularly those with physical disabilities – to show their talents, e.g. through the use of digital art, and through music technology.)

All-rounders

An 'all-rounder' is defined by the DfES as someone showing ability in *both the academic and the talent realms*. Another type of all-rounder is one who shows multiple skills within a particular talent area, e.g. Ian Botham, the cricketer, who was also of professional standard in other sports.

In both cases there are challenges involved.

The first challenge is **time**. Managing time is difficult for all pupils these days. For those with multiple gifts and talents, the pressures can be immense: parental and school expectations, and the commitment of time on a regular basis for developing and maintaining physical skills can be daunting. Think of the number of hours a 'serious' swimmer or ice-skater puts in – often two hours a day before school even starts! Time needs to be taken to build up stamina, whether in playing the violin, or developing the 'lip' needed for French horn, or the endurance to run the marathon. I have personal experience (during my History degree at university) of 'doing an all-nighter' to press forward with some unfinished coursework, due the next day. This simply isn't possible in many of the talent areas: if the long-term preparation is not there, if you are not 'in shape', then you can not 'deliver the goods', and may even be subject to physical injury.

The second challenge is **choices**. Which sport to devote one's energies to above all others? Which instrument to specialise in at music college? Whether to do a 'sensible' degree in mathematics or law, rather than risk a career in the arts? Which of two much-loved areas to make a commitment to?

Of course, some pupils take all this in their stride. I know a girl who is currently waiting the results of some interviews for higher education. To date, she has been offered a scholarship to one of the London music colleges, a place at an art college, and an academic place at a university…all in different subjects! Fortunately, she isn't flustered by this, approaching it all with a remarkably 'laid back' attitude.

This is not always the case, however, and it is important that schools realise that for many students these choices can be agonising; they can begin with frustration over limited GCSE choices, and can often take years to resolve.

CASE STUDY

Caroline is an exceptionally fine solo singer. A good all-round musician, she also plays piano to a high standard, and has been a member of an outstanding youth choir. All of her free time is spent in musical activities of one sort and another. Not surprisingly, she spent most of her secondary school years planning to study Music at university. In the sixth form, she began to study German seriously, and for the first time began to have doubts about Music as her number one choice. She agonised about the place of music in her life, wondering if it would best be kept as a rewarding pastime, rather than a pressured source of regular income.

In the end she decided to pursue a degree in German. But she and a friend spent her first Easter holiday at university staying in youth hostels, visiting opera houses in Italy! She may well go on to do a postgraduate diploma in singing. But the choices presented will not be resolved for some years to come.

Issues for schools: all-rounders

Time:

■ Be aware of the time pressures connected with a real commitment to a talent area. Long hours need to be spent in training, rehearsing, playing and performing. Schools can now 'personalise' pupil timetables to a much greater extent, to allow time for practice. (Hopefully this will become the norm, and not the exception.)

■ While schools are becoming more aware of the issue of staff workload, many have not yet tackled the issue of pupil workload. All-rounders who are struggling with mountains of homework and coursework are likely to feel particularly pressured.

Choices:

■ Be aware of the exceptional pressures talented pupils can feel when it comes to hard choices about how to spend their very limited time. Even decisions about how to spend the summer holidays can become dominated by conflicting interests: the family holiday or the intensive tennis camp? The orchestral course or the youth choir tour?

■ When counselling pupils over options (for GCSE, A-level and further/higher education) remember that they are wrestling with exceptionally difficult issues. For talented pupils their talent area is a means of self-expression which goes beyond mere 'interest' (see Chapter 8, 'Talented pupils').

INSET

- Schools are under continual pressure to raise and maintain pupils' academic achievements, often in line with strict 'targets'. This can result in subtle – and not-so-subtle – messages being given to pupils about which subjects are more 'valuable' than others. For example, special recognition may be being given for academic effort and achievement, but not for work in the arts or in sport. (Specialist colleges need to ensure that pupils whose talents do not coincide with the school's particular speciality still receive the support they need.)
- What effect might these messages be having on all-rounders, who may be facing very high expectations in terms of their academic work, while trying to systematically develop their talents in other areas?

An inclusive approach to talent-spotting

Identifying talented pupils

What do we mean by an inclusive approach to talent-spotting? In educational terms the term 'inclusion' originated in Special Education, where it referred to programmes designed to meet individual pupils' needs within the classroom alongside other pupils, rather than by removing them to take part in special programmes. Over time, the concept of inclusion in education has been broadened to include a more general philosophy of valuing and including students from every culture, valuing diversity, and overcoming barriers to the access and participation of particular groups of students.

We have already seen that pupils from homes which value the arts and sport are at a significant advantage in terms of their access to learning the basic skills needed for exceptional talent to show. We have also seen that because of the nature of the talent areas – dependent as they are on the development of physical skills – pupils without access to these opportunities will never become the early developers and prodigies that we so often look for in this area. Yet they may well have the potential to pursue their talents to a high level, either as a career, or as an enrichment to their lives.

An inclusive approach to talent-spotting is one which hopes to spread the net widely in the search for talent, overcoming barriers to achievement, providing opportunities to develop the necessary skills for their talents to show, and creating an environment in which all pupils can enjoy the benefits of participation in the talent realm.

The fundamental principle of an inclusive approach to talent-spotting is to provide opportunities on a sustained basis to as many pupils as possible, to create a wide base of participation from which talented pupils will emerge. It does not mean a lowering of standards or watering down of provision: it means a considered and systematic approach which recognises the whole range of issues connected with talent identification and talent development, including family background, task commitment, the need for good coaching, the investment of time needed to build up and maintain the physical skills involved, and so on.

Identifying talented pupils: strengths and weaknesses of commonly used methods

Before going on to look at some practical examples of this more inclusive approach, it is useful to review some of the methods commonly used by schools to identify pupils with high achievement or potential high achievement in the talent realm. The identification process sometimes takes place systematically, on a whole-school basis (e.g. as part of a formal effort to create a register of talented pupils), and at other times in an ongoing and less formal way (e.g. in selection procedures for a place on the school football team, for an art exhibition in the school hall or on the internet, for a part in the school play, membership of the school choir, and so on).

Typically, identification involves a variety of methods, including:

■ **Tests of 'ability'** – e.g. in music (the talent area with by far the most tests of this type). These would include the (now largely discredited) Bentley Tests of Musical Ability, plus a whole host of other attempts to test areas such as pitch discrimination, rhythm and so on. (For a thorough review of a number of tests of musical ability, see Shuter-Dyson and Gabriel 1981 and Sloboda 1985.) They also might include so-called tests of 'creativity', which have been shown to have less overall validity than those for intelligence.

While this kind of screening may result in identifying some pupils with unrecognised ability, there is no general agreement as to which test or tests are the most valid. There are also serious concerns about issues such as cultural bias. In the end, they probably test attainment and prior knowledge rather more than aptitude.

At a deeper level, some writers feel that the use of 'ability tests' simply reinforces the commonly held view that talent is something that only 'runs in families'. Certainly in music, this can have a discouraging effect on those not blessed with a 'musical background':

> traditional concepts of 'musical' people having some special genetic predisposition to music have often tended to undermine the confidence of beginners and deterred others from even starting...I have...lost count of the number of students I have taken for private instrumental tuition who were initially turned down by their school on the grounds that they had failed a musical ability test or were considered 'unmusical'. Some of these students went on to achieve a remarkably high standard in performance.
>
> (Murphy 2002, p. 67)

■ **Tests of performance** – e.g. competitions, auditions and trial periods. These primarily test attainment, and in the case of the performing arts and sport, they also test confidence and the ability to perform under pressure.

There is some justification for using these procedures, since they mimic the pressures performers will face in real life. (The number of aspiring opera singers, fine artists, actors and Premier League footballers far exceeds the number of opportunities to make a career in these areas.) Trial periods (e.g. where a pupil joins a performing group or team for a few sessions to see how they cope and how they fit in) can be useful in some situations. For instance, a young player might be asked to train with older pupils on a trial basis, to see how his skills compare. (As a youngster, the footballer David Beckham regularly played with groups of more 'advanced' players. He felt this prepared him for the kind of competition he would find at professional level.)

However, on the negative side, there is a danger of confusing *performance* with *ability*. For example, primary school children are sometimes 'tested' for places in the instrumental tuition programme by being asked to sing back a complex melody or clap back a lengthy rhythm. Those who can do this successfully are chosen for, say, violin lessons, even if they are not particularly interested in playing the violin. This means that if a child is not accustomed to singing regularly, they are at a serious disadvantage: in other words, it is a test of performance and not of ability. (I'm terrible at clapping back a rhythm, and would certainly have failed this particular test!)

CASE STUDY

'One-off' tests of confidence can be deceptive. A child who is a perfectionist about their performance can end up doing less well 'on the day'. I recall a very talented pianist whom I adjudicated in a festival recently. She was clearly the most 'musical' of the performers in the sense of her involvement in the music. But she had chosen a piece far beyond her capabilities. In the end there was plenty of commitment but far too many wrong notes, and she failed to place in the competition. Her 'audition' certainly did not show her true ability.

■ **Recommendations** from the teachers, parents and peers of talented youngsters. This can be a particularly useful way of finding out about out-of-school achievements, and I've several times had letters from parents of rather shy youngsters, letting me know that their son or daughter was achieving at a high level in music lessons outside school. Usually parents are very keen that their children's gifts be appreciated, and it is useful for the teachers to know of their pupils' sometimes well-hidden talents. (The danger, of course, is that it may also 'identify' those with over-involved parents!)

CASE STUDY

A young teacher received a special needs information sheet about a boy joining one of her Year 7 classes from another form. He was described as isolated socially, and given to serious outbursts of temper and frustration. His parents shared with the school the information that the boy was working on Grade 5 Piano at home – an achievement well above the norm for his age. By alerting the teacher to his talent, she was able to encourage him to contribute in music classes. Once he had been able to share – very shyly – his interest and exceptional ability in music, he became co-operative and willing to join in group activities.

- **National curriculum guidelines** for spotting potential high achievers in Physical Education, Music and Art. These provide a very useful starting point, especially for non-specialist teachers, in identifying some of the characteristics which might indicate exceptional talent. However, there are some drawbacks, since pupils are seldom 'typical'. (For the current National Curriculum guidelines for Identifying Talented Pupils in Art, Physical Education and Music, see Appendix B.)

  For example, the guidelines for music emphasise the ability to *memorise music quickly without any apparent effort*. One of my voice students is an outstanding all-round musician. Currently aged 17, he attends the Royal Academy of Music Junior Academy, where his aural work and general musicianship are regarded as outstanding. Although he can fluently 'sing at sight' almost any piece of vocal music, he finds it almost impossible to memorise his songs!

- **Transition information** from primary schools is beginning to be handed on to secondary schools in a more systematic and consistent way. However, in some cases this fails to mention talent activities which are taking place outside school. In dealing with the transition from primary to secondary school of youngsters already identified as showing exceptional talent, it is also important to balance high expectations with the awareness that some children who performed confidently in primary school may develop a crippling self-consciousness in secondary school.

- **Informal questionnaires** – these can be very useful in identifying both potential and achievement in the talent areas, both inside school and in external clubs and private tuition. It is also one way to access information about 'musical', 'sporting' and 'artistic' homes.

  One effective way to collect informal information about activities outside school (to aid in identification, and to amplify transition information) is by using simple strategies such as asking children to write about their activities, using a simple 'Music/Art/Sport in my life' format (see Figure 7.1). This simple exercise (which can be done with each class in the first lesson of the year) should include more general questions, such as 'What sport (or type of music, or kinds of artwork) do you most enjoy watching/playing/etc.?' This avoids dividing the class into 'sheep and goats', i.e. those who have had tuition and those who have not. Results should be confidential, to avoid embarrassing anyone.

  Note: The questions about the home can yield useful results: I once found that a Year 9 girl had a tuba at her home, which her brother had once had lessons on but had given up. She took up the tuba, and became a fine player.

Music in my life

What music do you enjoy listening to at home?

Does anyone in your family play an instrument?

Are there any musical instruments at your home?

Music lessons at school usually include **performing**, **composing** and **listening to music**. Which of these activities do you enjoy the most?

The least?

Do you like to sing?

Have you ever sung in a choir (either inside or outside school)?

Do you play any instruments, e.g. recorder, violin, guitar, keyboard, harmonium?

Have you had any lessons on any instruments (either inside or outside school)?

Is there an instrument that you have always wanted to learn?

Have you ever been to a 'live' concert? Who was performing in it?

Figure 7.1 An informal method for gathering information about out-of-school activities

■ **Physical characteristics** are an important element in selection in sport, in dance and, to some extent, in music (where matching embouchure to instrument can be an important element). In some sports, studies have taken place which measure physical attributes in a systematic way, hoping to define an 'ideal profile' for the sport. For example, the KASP Study (Carter and Ackland 1994) measured 1,050 athletes attending the World Aquatic Championships in 1994, analysing their height, the length of their body segments, their body mass, girth, skinfold thickness, and so on. This showed significant differences between swimmers in different events (e.g. breast-stroke, freestyle, etc.), and differences between the 'elite performers' and 'the rest'.

In practice, though, this kind of systematically collected information about physical characteristics can be difficult to translate into talent identification at school level. The basis of this approach is that there is an 'ideal' physical profile which is an important aspect of success. However, these characteristics vary with age and are particularly unstable during adolescence, making early identification of elite performers difficult. It also fails to take account of all the other elements which contribute to success – training regimes, psychological attitude, and so on. Above all, this research focuses exclusively on 'elite performance', rather than on the group of athletes who have gained much from their experience but have perhaps not reached the very top. An academic review sponsored by SportScotland in 2002 found that 'the key determinants of potential are largely psychological' and recommended that resources currently concentrated on anthropometrical measures should instead be focused on psychological dimensions, supported by development of fundamental motor skills (SportScotland 2002, para. 31.5).

CASE STUDY

The use of physical measurement as the basis for selecting pupils for specialist training is probably seen at its most extreme in the current initiative known as **World Class Start**, currently being funded by Sport England.

The **World Class Start** programme aims to identify potential world-class performers in sports such as competitive rowing. Projects begin with a team of coaches visiting local schools, in the words of one girl, 'looking for The Stars of Tomorrow'. Various measurements are taken – weight, height, arm span, size of hands, and so on. Later on potential rowers receive a letter saying they have results 'similar to those of Olympic rowers' at their age. They are then invited to commit to a long-term training programme (of several years) to learn how to row competitively.

Only time will tell whether schemes such as this will produce elite performers in rowing; and there might be some concerns about signing youngsters up for long-term commitments in sports where they have little or no knowledge or experience.

Some students feel flattered to be 'chosen' and thrive on the new programmes. Others are less enthusiastic: as one of my bassoon students (whose school had been visited by one of the pilot projects) said: 'I'm tall, I have big hands and a wide arm span; my Dad rowed competitively and still coaches rowing; I'm the ideal candidate...but I'd rather play the bassoon!'

Issues for schools

Existing methods of identifying talented pupils have both strengths and weaknesses when applied to a school setting. Many of the approaches – particularly in sport – are designed specifically to identify 'elite performers' or 'world-class athletes'. (There may be few of these in your school.) Some methods appear to be very scientific (e.g. tests of musical perception devised by psychologists, anthropometric tests for sport) without acknowledging other important aspects of talent development such as motivation. Still other models tend to identify attainment rather than potential.

An approach based on using a combination of different methods (e.g. teacher recommendation, tests, parental recommendation, National Curriculum guidelines, attainment as measured by membership of County or Area groups) is likely to be more effective than focusing solely on one model.

However, existing methods fail to take account of an essential element in talent identification and development: exceptional performance is the result of a long process of lessons, practice and encouragement (SportScotland 2002). Unless youngsters are offered these opportunities – in as inclusive a way as is practicable – many will find their talents are overlooked.

A more inclusive approach to talent-spotting

Owing to the nature of talent development – and, in particular, the need for sustained training and exposure to the talent area – many of the current models for talent identification tend to over-identify those from homes which nurture particular talents. A parent who is very interested in sport will make a special effort to ensure that their child receives the best possible coaching, and may drive miles to take them to a special programme in tennis, or swimming. In fact the child may not themselves be particularly interested, but especially in the primary and early secondary school years, they will follow the parents' lead.

Attempts to overcome this bias in provision (e.g. through workshops and 'taster' sessions) can be helpful in revealing those with an 'instant aptitude' for an activity; but the youngster who shows him or herself to be outstanding in a workshop situation is often already interested in other pursuits, or is simply 'good at everything'. As a result, these kinds of 'one off' events can fail to identify those who would benefit most from provision for specialist coaching, and other opportunities to develop their skills.

Like a duck to water?

All of the talent areas are particularly dependent on the development of physical skills. It takes time (and good coaching) to develop these skills sufficiently for exceptional talent to show. Take, for example, show jumping. A child's first attempts at riding a horse are only the first steps towards developing the confidence and experience necessary to handle the animal well. Only then can they begin to tackle complex movements and eventually become confident at attempting a jump. By the time real talent in show jumping shows itself, a very long period of gestation has gone by. A weekend 'crash course' in riding is unlikely to be sufficient to reveal all of those who will go on to show talent in show jumping. And while some who take to things like ducks to water will definitely go on to develop their newly found talents, many will not.

I remember reading a 'letter to the editor' in a professional journal for musicians (*ISM* (Incorporated Society of Musicians) *Journal*, August 2003), where a professional oboist told how he 'took to' the oboe at the age of nine, and progressed to a career as a professional player. However, I also remember a student of mine who made a spectacularly good sound on the oboe, at the very first attempt to play; but she didn't have the interest and dedication to continue beyond the first lesson!

We need a vision of discovering talent which is more sustained and more inclusive, casting our net as widely as possible in order to unlock untapped potential for achievement in these areas. The first important element in this is to ensure adequate, sustained provision to opportunities and training.

To recap:

- Success in the talent areas is heavily dependent on the development of a range of **physical skills**.

- This development requires a particularly heavy input of **time, training and experience**, to build muscle memory, overcome 'performance nerves', and gain the experience needed to make the most of these skills. For example, young footballers need to have a balance of time spent in developing skills and in participating in actual games; young actors need to be 'seasoned' by a series of performances (including some occasions where things don't go according to plan!).[1]

- Although some pupils will 'take to' a talent area like the proverbial duck to water, in most cases pupils will need training and experience on a **sustained** basis, in order to reveal their potential in a talent area.

- Since **task commitment** is such an important element in talent development, it is important to identify those pupils who have the necessary interest, dedication and sheer enjoyment to devote to their talent area. This does not necessarily mean that they have to love the 'purposeful practice' discussed by the writers on

---

1 In sport, some have argued that here in the UK too much emphasis is placed on game experience and not enough on skills development. Whatever the balance is, there is no doubt that both experiences are needed.

Expert Performance. In many cases talented youngsters will be reluctant to practise. But they must at least gain some satisfaction from playing, dancing, singing, swimming, acting and so forth (see Chapter 8, 'Talented pupils').

In other words we need a systematic approach, based on some clear principles:

- **offering maximum access to training and other opportunities,**
- combined with **high standards,**
- and an **emphasis on psychological factors, such as task commitment.**

Provision before identification: the importance of sustained provision

In light of this, clearly the best overall approach to talent identification is:

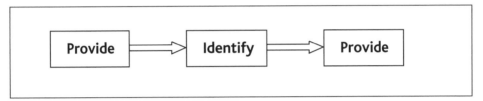

Figure 7.2

However, this does not fully show the importance of *the initial provision phase*. In reality, our diagram should look like this:

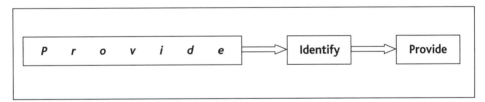

Figure 7.3

In a more inclusive approach to talent-spotting, the identification phase needs to be delayed, preferably until after a sustained period of provision. This way we can ensure a level playing field for pupils who do not have the benefit of an early start.

With this approach, master classes, short courses and one-off events have their place. But only if followed up with more *sustained opportunities* to develop the skills necessary for pupils' talents to show.

An inclusive approach in practice

Let us look at some practical examples of this kind of sustained provision, leading to identification, and coupled with approaches which reward task commitment and perseverance and motivation.

Music

> **CASE STUDY**
>
> In my first teaching post I had the good fortune to find myself in a large comprehensive, with a large music department.
>
> At that time, instrumental lessons were fully funded by the county. However, the downside was that this made for a limited pot of funding – it wasn't possible for parents to purchase time directly from teachers if lists were full. This particular school happened to have a cupboard full of unused orchestral instruments. But as a result of the shortfall in teaching time, there seemed to be no way to put these instruments to good use.
>
> It was decided to offer pupils the opportunity to learn these instruments from scratch in an after-school programme modelled on methods in use in the United States (where virtually all school-based instrumental teaching takes place on a whole-class basis). American band method instruction books were purchased for a range of instruments, volunteers were recruited from Year 7, and the group lessons were also offered to those in Years 8 and 9 who were on waiting lists for instrumental tuition.
>
> The plan was to meet after school on a weekly basis, after some initial sessions with individuals to show them the basics of how to make a sound, how to put the instrument together, and so on. Since the Junior Band rehearsals took place after school, parents had to give their consent and co-operation, and make arrangements to see the children home safely.
>
> Soon it was a thriving group from which several good players began to emerge. As instrumental teaching time became available (for example, as other pupils gave up, or left the school), those who had proven to be the most capable players – and reliable attendees – were given lessons in addition to their band work. In time, several of them went on to play in the County Youth Orchestra, and some became professional musicians.

Sport

> **CASE STUDY**
>
> Much later in my teaching career, I was Director of Music at a boys' school in Lincolnshire. Although a relatively small school, it had a national reputation for water polo – a surprising achievement, especially as they didn't have a swimming pool!
>
> I was curious about how this outstanding team – which featured annually in national competitions – had developed, particularly as some of my young musicians were also involved, arriving late for before-school rehearsals with their heads wet from swimming. I was surprised to find that the activity took place entirely outside school hours and off the premises. The Head of ICT (who also sang in my school choir!) was in charge of the programme, which used the local swimming baths for training.
>
> Apparently, boys who wanted to be on the team simply turned up for the early morning practice session, which were open to everyone who wanted to come along and train. When the time came to pick teams to represent the school in competitions, choices were made from among the regular attendees. A 'prima donna' with lots of ability but poor attendance was unlikely to make the team; instead, the coach would choose a youngster who had made the effort to develop his skills on a regular basis throughout his time at the school.

Drama

> **CASE STUDY**
>
> A teacher at a local school in my neighbourhood decided to start a drama group in the community. He and his wife were heavily involved in a high-profile amateur theatre group in town, and wanted to share their enthusiasm and expertise. The ten-year-old son of a friend of mine was looking for something to do in the summer, and decided to give it a try.
>
> The group was open access, with no audition required and only a small fee involved, to cover expenses. Children learned 'the basics' of acting, with lessons in stage movement, in make-up, and in speaking lines clearly. Those who were regular attendees were all involved in the workshop activities, with opportunities to develop acting skills across a range of roles, both leading and supporting. Extended productions (given for parents and friends) were chosen with a view to involving every child in some way. Formal auditions were avoided and regular attendees 'rewarded' with leading roles in productions.
>
> Geoff's parents (both musicians) led busy lives as teachers, performers and conductors, and like all of my musical friends, had made sure both their sons had begun to learn

instruments at an early age. (By the age of ten both boys were competent players on at least two instruments.)

They were intrigued when their son began to show more and more interest in his drama group, and proud and delighted when he began to be selected for leading roles in the troupe. He began to attend summer schools offered by the National Youth Music Theatre, and by the age of 13 had played Bottom in a full production of Shakespeare's *A Midsummer Night's Dream*. By the time he reached 16, he had decided to pursue a career as an actor.

What do these successful schemes for discovering talent have in common?

- All were **inclusive**. No formal selection was involved before youngsters were allowed to engage in regular training. In the Junior Band, the number of pupils interested happened to correspond fairly well with the number of instruments available; so, with some trying out of instruments and shifting around, it worked out well. And the percussion section proved to be infinitely expandable, to accommodate any extras who were waiting for instruments to become available.

- Because the activity was **offered on a sustained basis** pupils had a chance to develop their skills, and – in the case of late starters, or those who lacked a home background in the talent area – to make up lost ground. Those who volunteered enthusiastically at the beginning were not always those who stayed the course. So although the activities were 'open access', those who were not 'serious' about the activity soon dropped out, leaving a core of those with the necessary interest and enthusiasm to achieve some measure of success.

- All were **sociable** activities, with a group of youngsters working together towards a common goal, and operating with **clear rules and expectations governing membership**. This resulted in more motivation, a clear sense of identity, and friendships which developed across age ranges, based on a common interest. Practising complex skills in isolation from others can be a daunting task. Working in a group can make all the difference. The *informal competition* which comes through training with a club or organisation also serves as a useful 'trial run' for the competition which naturally accompanies many of the talent areas; e.g. 'working one's way up the section' as a clarinetist, and having to 'deliver the goods' in an audition or in rehearsals and concerts, is good preparation for a future in which auditions for places in orchestras and bands are the norm.

- Active **parental involvement** was there from the first. I know from personal experience that my private students – whose parents have made a commitment to arrange for the lessons outside school, to select a teacher, and to provide transport outside schools hours – have generally been more motivated and continued with their lessons longer than those whom I've taught on an individual or small group basis in schools. Close contact with parents means that youngsters have the support needed to succeed; and also that when plateaus of achievement arrive, parents are on hand to encourage pupils to continue through the 'difficult patch'.

Successful approaches to talent identification and development are therefore seen to combine:

- Inclusivity
- Sustained provision
- A sociable/group element
- Parental involvement

(see Figure 7.4).

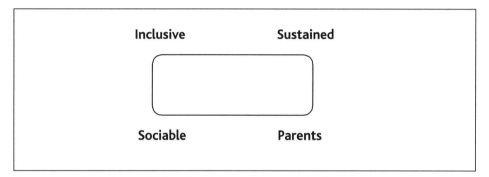

Figure 7.4 An inclusive model for talent identification and development

Inclusivity in action: the Sheffield Project

The Sheffield Project provides a more detailed example of how the *Inclusive Model for Talent Identification* (Figure 7.4) has worked out in practice: this time, over a range of different primary schools.

The aim was to identify Year 5 pupils at inner-city (*EiC*) primary schools who might benefit the most from a series of 'taster lessons' delivered by the Music Service. Since funds were limited, selection was needed. Youngsters were 'selected' over an extended period of time, using a range of methods designed to test their task commitment and interest as well as their initial ability. Parental involvement was an important element, with materials being designed to help both parents and pupils to have a realistic view of what was involved in learning an instrument.

For a full description of the project, and copies of the materials used, see Appendix C.

Issues for schools: the value of an inclusive approach

The term 'talent-spotting' implies that talent is something innate – a special attribute bestowed on the favoured few; and that this special quality can somehow be identified, through a range of tests and measurements, through recommendation by 'experts' who can 'spot' potential in a given area, through success in a 'talent competition'. We readily say 'She is so talented!' or 'He has a real talent for gymnastics', because we can see that their performance is above the usual level for their age, and/or that there seems to be a special indefinable 'flair', enjoyment and engagement in their approach.

Yet as we've seen, identifying talented pupils – especially those whose talents are as yet unrecognised and undeveloped – is a much more challenging business altogether. An inclusive approach can simplify difficult decisions about the use of scarce resources, encourage healthy competition, and reward task commitment. It can also serve to open doors for those who for a variety of reasons have lacked the opportunity to discover their hidden talents.

Identification and selection are facts of life

Schools are regularly asked to identify pupils with talents in sport and in the arts. This may be for a 'register of gifted and talented pupils', to represent the school in a sports team, to be put on a waiting list for instrumental music lessons, or simply to have their work exhibited in the foyer on Open Day. The selection may be made on a whole-school basis, within departments, or by individuals in charge of extracurricular groups. Some may be highly aware of the issues involved in the education of gifted and talented pupils; others will be specialists in other areas.

Whoever makes these decisions, it is important that they be informed ones. The aim is to motivate and encourage all pupils to develop their talents, and to do our best to identify both those with undiscovered talent and underachievers.

INSET

1. What approaches does your school currently use to identify talented pupils?

    - Testing procedures applied across a year group
    - Teacher recommendation
    - Peer recommendation
    - Parental recommendation
    - Transfer information from primary school
    - Informal questionnaires

2. How do you go about finding out about pupils' **talents which are being developed outside school**?

    - Informal methods, e.g. by asking them to write about 'Music/Sport/ Drama/Art in my life'
    - Peer recommendation
    - Parental recommendation
    - Transfer information from primary school

3. Consider the model for a more inclusive approach to talent identification shown in Figure 7.4. How might you implement aspects of the model, either on its own or in conjunction with other methods?
4. Which members of staff in your school are responsible, either directly or indirectly, for identifying talented pupils, e.g. by selecting for sports teams, art exhibits, plays, musicals, concerts and so on? How might you go about raising their awareness of some of the issues involved in identifying talented pupils – particularly those whose talents have not yet been recognised?

CHAPTER 8

Talented pupils

The excellence of every art is its intensity...

(John Keats, in a letter to his brother, December 1817)

Introduction

We are all in the business of trying to motivate and support pupils to make the best of their gifts and talents, whether in their academic studies or in the arts and sport. Certainly in my experience of working with schools, LEAs and groups of Gifted and Talented/Able Pupil Coordinators, the three most frequently asked questions are:

- What are talented pupils like?
- What are their distinctive needs?
- How can we best support our talented pupils?

This chapter focuses on the pupils themselves and asks the question, 'What are talented pupils like?' Chapters 9 and 10 ('The talent-enhancing school') look in more detail at some of the distinctive needs of talented pupils, and suggest a number of practical strategies for supporting talented pupils in our schools.

What does it mean to be talented?

Why is there so much confusion and mystery surrounding what it means to be talented?

To some extent this is part of a mind-set in which talents are thought of as mysterious things, bestowed from above, and that talented people are therefore something different from the norm; whereas I would argue that, on the contrary, many people have talents that would have shown themselves if only the opportunities to develop them had been offered more inclusively (see Chapter 7, 'An inclusive approach to talent-spotting').

Another reason for feeling that talented people are 'a breed apart' may simply be that for a variety of reasons the arts and sport tend to be under-represented in terms of senior management posts in schools. This means that the people in charge of making important decisions and setting up systems in schools may have little or no knowledge of what it means to have a particular talent.

Deborah Eyre, author of the important book *Able Children in Ordinary Schools* (1997), argues that able children are just like other children. They encompass the full range of personality types, physical characteristics, home backgrounds and so on – everything which makes them the individuals that all children are.

This is also true of talented pupils, who run the full gamut of personality traits, home backgrounds and approaches to school and work.

Some talented pupils

CASE STUDY 1

Grace and Rebecca are both in the Lower Sixth at their respective comprehensive schools, which are known for their music provision. Both girls are talented violinists, who hope to go on to music college after their A-levels and to make their careers in music. Both tackle their music-making with a real intensity; yet their temperaments couldn't be more different.

Grace is reliable, positive and easy to work with. Although music is her first love (she regularly arrives at school at 7.30 a.m. to get some extra practice in before classes begin), she is equally talented in art, and is also near the top of her year group academically. She is very active in extracurricular music at her school, singing in the Chamber Choir, playing the flute in the Concert Band, violin in the Chamber Strings, and keyboards in the Jazz Band. Despite being heavily involved in County Music Service performing groups, and keeping up with her lessons in piano, flute and violin, her coursework is always in on time, and of a good standard. She is an exceptional player, with great attention to detail, coupled with a real ability to 'move' people with her commitment to the music.

Rebecca is also a violinist – in fact she was something of a prodigy, performing to a very high standard at an early age. In primary school she enjoyed performing solos at school events such as Awards Evening; now that she is in secondary school she has become reluctant to play in public, and no amount of coaxing will encourage her to do a solo in assembly. Rebecca is totally disorganised in every area of her life. She is frequently late for lessons, never hands her homework in on time (even in music) and, despite being well above average in academic ability, her coursework is usually slapdash. (Her teachers find her irritating in the extreme – a real frustration to teach.) She is very active in County groups, and is currently near the top of the First Violin section in the Youth Orchestra, which frequently performs at the Schools Prom in London. She feels that the school groups are of a poor standard in comparison with the County groups, and takes part only reluctantly. In fact, she feels the school 'doesn't understand' her, and longs to attend another school locally, where there are more young musicians. Increasingly, she is getting involved in the local pop music scene, playing guitar in a band, and staying out all hours. Her parents are very supportive, but are increasingly worried about her behaviour both in and out of school.

CASE STUDY 2

Steven is in Year 9 at an inner-city comprehensive, and is a talented footballer. He has has just been selected to be on the City football squad. Steven has his problems at school, especially in his academic lessons, where he frequently exhibits challenging behaviour. A kinaesthetic learner, he finds it particularly difficult to concentrate in subjects such as English, which rely mainly on written work. His behaviour in PE – his favourite subject – is entirely different. Here, he is allowed to take the lead and to mentor pupils by helping them to develop their skills. When Steven's name comes up at staff meetings (usually in connection with his poor attitude, bad behaviour and failure to hand in homework), the PE teachers find it difficult to recognise the Steven that they know to be conscientious, keen and eager to help out, even with dull tasks such as putting away equipment after practices.

CASE STUDY 3

James is a highly talented artist. In his primary school he's known to be difficult to handle. He frequently refuses to work with other pupils, and has a reputation for being awkward with his class teacher. Determined to 'go his own way', he refuses to ask for help when he's confronted with a piece of academic work. This means that in spite of being quite able, academically, his achievement lags well behind his potential. James's mother is a trained artist, and encourages James to explore a range of media. Since he was very small, she has arranged for him to attend a variety of art classes, and has broadened his general experience by taking him to art exhibitions on a regular basis. In his out-of-school art activities he is a model participant: keen, co-operative, sociable and respectful. He even asks for help and advice when needed! His mother finds this contrast in behaviour very upsetting. School parents' evenings are a particular frustration, as she struggles to convince school staff that her son is not a problem outside school. She's hoping that when he moves to the local secondary school (which is a specialist Arts College) that his unco-operative behaviour will change; but she's worried that patterns of underachievement (particularly in his academic work) may prove hard to overcome.

The advantages of this variety

It would be astounding if all talented pupils were the same. In fact it would be counter-productive.

We all know of the saying 'All chiefs and no Indians'. If all young sportsmen wanted to be goal-scorers, there would be no one in defence; if all violinists wanted to be Paganini, there would be no 'rank and file' second violins (and probably no violas at all, since their role is almost entirely a supporting one); if all wind players wanted to play melodies most of the time, there would be plenty of flutes and clarinets, but no tubas or bass trombones; if all dancers became Principals, we would have no *corps de ballet*; without someone to set the pace, Roger Bannister wouldn't have broken the four-minute barrier in running the mile. We *need* a variety of temperaments and approaches to field a sports team, play or sing ensemble music, produce a balanced cast for a play.

Issues for schools

- *Avoid stereotyping talented pupils, e.g. by assuming that pupils with talent in sport will all be confident and popular, or that 'artists' will be dreamy, actors 'difficult', etc. As with academically able children, there is no one pattern or personality which invariably applies.*
- *If we believe, for example, that all young actors will be moody and 'difficult' we run the risk of encouraging pupils to live up to that stereotype. This will not be helpful to them in the long run; if they go on to pursue a career in acting, they will soon find out that 'prima donnas' are not welcome.*
- *If a talented pupil is showing challenging behaviour, it's easy to blame it on the 'artistic temperament', whereas in fact it may simply be because the school is not supporting the pupil appropriately.*

INSET

Think of one talented pupil you know, and quickly jot down some words to describe his or her personality – lively, difficult, dreamy, confident, anxious and so on. (Make a note of their particular talent area – music, art, sport, drama, creative writing, etc.)

If you are working with colleagues, first do this exercise individually and then compare notes in a 'brainstorming' session. You can include talented pupils you know outside the school (perhaps in your own family), or focus on those within your particular school context.

This activity can be extended by asking colleagues to focus in turn on each of the talent areas (sport, performing arts, visual arts), exploring their preconceptions about 'typical' pupils.

While many sports and creative arts activities focus on 'solo performing' (e.g. tennis, many areas of fine art, competitive swimming), others allow for a range of roles, e.g. the leading actors in a play, compared with those who make a career in supporting roles; or the Leader of the First Violins (who will relish the pressure of playing solo parts on a regular basis), in contrast with the Second Bassoonist, who enjoys playing musically, but without being in the limelight.

Gifts and talents

Much time and energy can be spent debating whether or not academic giftedness and talent are one and the same (see Chapter 2, '"Academic" gifts and "non-academic" talents').

Like academically gifted pupils, talented pupils tend to be **extremely focused on their talent area**, sometimes with a single-mindedness and sheer intensity which verges on obsession. When this obsessive interest is coupled with the heavy investment of time and energy (often outside school hours) in training and performing, the commitment can be all-consuming.

And like their academically gifted counterparts, they also need the **company of their peers**. In fact, in some cases, talent development is next to impossible without it, for instance in team-based sports, drama, dance and ensemble playing. (For a fuller discussion of the implications of this in school terms, see Chapters 9 and 10, 'The talent-enhancing school'.)

However, both my personal experience of working with (and in fact being part of) both groups – the academically gifted and the talented – leads me to believe strongly that there is an added dimension to understanding talented pupils. This is to do with the talent area's function as both an *emotional and physical outlet*, and its links with *identity* and *self-worth*.

The relationship of a talented individual to his or her area of talent can be very intense. Talented pupils *need* to draw, act, sing, play, skate, swim and so forth. When this is withdrawn, they can suffer serious depression.

This may be because talented people differ from the norm in that they express an important part of their personality through their talent area. Just as most of us express ourselves in words (and would be devastated at the loss of our speech and the ability to communicate with others), a dancer expresses him or herself with their body, through dance. If this outlet for self-expression is removed for some reason – either by injury, or even through seemingly minor events such as not being allowed to attend an important rehearsal – a true dancer can become despondent and difficult.

Talent and personality: the artistic temperament and the athletic personality

We often speak of talented pupils as having an 'artistic temperament', by which we mean a heightened sensitivity, both to emotions and to physical surroundings.

CASE STUDY

Stephanie is very talented in art. When her family moved to a new house, she refused to move into the bedroom allocated to her, and instead insisted on sleeping on the settee in the lounge. This went on for several days. Finally the parents got to the bottom of the problem: the new room was painted a bright shade of lime green. She was so sensitive to colour, that she couldn't bear to be in a room with that shade of green. They repainted the room (a soothing taupe!) and she moved happily from the settee into her new bedroom.

To most of us this seems extreme. To an artistically talented pupil, it makes perfect sense: although most of us are affected by colour, her emotions were affected so strongly that she was unable to use the room at all.

The 'artistic temperament'

It is certainly true that the community of artists, writers, musicians and actors seems to have more than its fair share of mental instability and suicide, often coupled with a bohemian lifestyle. In fact there is convincing evidence that artists are more likely to suffer from bipolar affective disorder (commonly known as manic depression), and tend to be more prone to suicide in later life. In her book *Touched with Fire: Manic Depressive Illness and the Artistic Temperament* Kay Redfield Jamison – herself a manic depressive – examines the lives of an impressively long list of artists (fine artists, authors and composers) whose lives were marked by bipolar disorder.[1] Others have seen a link between cyclothymic disorder and obsessive compulsive disorder and the so-called 'artistic temperament'.

Of course, the main danger in trying to define an artistic temperament is that we run the risk of stereotyping people with interests in the arts. While it is true that a disproportionate number may suffer from mood disorders, the majority will not.

However, it is useful to be aware of some of the characteristics people associate with the so-called artistic personality type. These include:

- frequent mood swings and heightened emotional reactivity;
- experiencing a greater range of emotion than 'ordinary' people, i.e. higher 'highs' and lower 'lows';
- times of great creativity and high quantity of work, alternating with significant periods of inactivity and inability to complete projects;
- lack of inhibition, and a tendency towards impulsiveness;
- heightened perceptions and senses, e.g. to colour or sound;
- an alternation between introversion and extraversion, sociability and solitude;
- a tendency to hide emotions beneath a tough exterior.

---

1   She also points out some disturbing research findings relating to bipolar disorder, e.g. that over their lifetime 46 per cent of patients with manic-depressive illness were involved in alcohol abuse and dependence, compared with 13 per cent of the general population. In the case of drug abuse, the lifetime prevalence in bipolar patients is 41 per cent, compared with 6 per cent in the general population (Redfield Jamison 1996, pp. 38–9).

Although, again, it is important to avoid stereotyping those with interests in the creative arts, it is also true that some of these preconceptions ring true in dealing with pupils whose talents lie in the arts (including writers and poets as well as those in music, art, drama and dance).

The 'athletic personality'

In sport, considerable research has been devoted to trying to identify personality differences between athletes and the general population. One aim of this has been to try to predict athletic success by using personality profiles as a means of selection for teams and training programmes. The research has looked at a number of different sports, and examined the differences between solo and team sports, and between contact sports and other sports such as athletics. For example, Morgan (1980) identified something that he termed the 'Iceberg Profile', which he argued was typical of most successful athletes. The more successful athletes had higher levels of vigour and lower levels of tension and depression than the less successful athletes.

Other studies have focused on the differences between athletes and non-athletes, in terms of aggression, anxiety and so on; while others have looked at the personality differences between more successful and less successful athletes within a particular sport. Still others have questioned whether these personality differences have arisen because of people's involvement in a particular sport, or whether particular sports simply attract different types of people!

While this work has not resulted in a generally accepted 'athletic personality type', there does seem to be some agreement that athletes in general are more emotional stable and more extraverted than non-athletes. This is in sharp contrast with the research evidence on the 'artistic temperament' and probably should be borne in mind by those dealing with young people who are involved in the arts and sport.

Some coaches and trainers have attempted to use Morgan's findings in an inappropriate way, using personality tests as means of selecting athletes for training programmes. However, most experts agree that this is a potentially dangerous practice.

Factors such as 'coachability', concentration, coping with adversity (an important element in task commitment), and effective mental preparation are much more important contributors to superior performance in sport.

Issues for schools
Research shows that people who are involved in the arts and sport may well have distinctive personality profiles.

- *It is important to be aware of this, particularly in dealing with the occasional pupil who may be suffering extremes of mood or showing early signs of bipolar disorders such as manic depression and cyclothymia.*
- *However, it is equally important not to stereotype pupils. Mood swings are not an invariable sign of artistic talent, and extraversion is not the hallmark of every sportsman/woman, particularly in adolescence.*

■ *It is generally agreed that attempting to identify pupils as 'talented' on the basis of personality type is potentially a dangerous practice.*

Talent as a physical and emotional outlet

The talent areas all involve an important physical element: artists speak of the sheer, visceral pleasure of drawing a flourish with a well-inked pen; musicians of making a beautiful sound on an instrument; sports men and women of the 'buzz' of hitting a particularly good shot at tennis. Removing this outlet can have a significant effect on attitude and behaviour.

CASE STUDY

Richard sang in the choir at school. Since the choir was involved in competitions and performances outside school, the heavy rehearsal schedule at certain times of the year meant he was singing almost every day of the school week. His mother reported that Richard – who was known to have a powerful temper – was 'a different child' when the choir was rehearsing regularly. The almost daily rehearsals had a noticeable effect: the outbursts of temper disappeared, he slept better, and was altogether a much happier and more productive child. Singing – which links the left and right sides of the brain – was having a physical effect.

Talent as a focus of identity and self-worth

For a talented pupil their area of talent is not just 'an activity', or 'something to do in my spare time', or even 'a possible career choice'. It is a vital part of their identity and sense of self-worth. For the truly talented, to be a 'musician', an 'actor', an 'artist', a 'gymnast' becomes part of their persona in a way that transcends the experience of those who just participate as a pleasant way of letting off steam, or meeting friends. The challenge for teachers and coaches is to identify those children for whom their talent area is not just an enjoyable pastime, but *essential* for their emotional well-being.

The same holds true for sport: emotional well-being is closely linked to the ability to perform, and in the case of high-profile athletes, it is a major source of identity and feelings of self-worth. Researchers at the University of North Carolina's Center for the Study of Retired Athletes (Bee 2003) interviewed almost 2,500 former National Football League players. While the study focused on the physical after-effects of a career in this particularly 'physical' contact sport, an interesting statistic also emerged with regard to the sports people whose marriages or relationships had broken down. In 50 per cent of these cases, the break-up had occurred in the first year after they had stopped competing. The emotional effects of losing the ability to compete also included clinical depression, and even suicide.

This also applies to athletes of school age. A 1995 Mayo Clinic study looked in detail at the cases of five young athletes who had attempted suicide after sustaining a serious injury which prevented them from playing (see NATA 1995 for details). The researchers found that seriously injured student athletes between the ages of 15 and 24 may be at increased risk of depression and possibly even suicide. The five injured athletes who attempted suicide following injuries shared the following characteristics:

- considerable athletic success before sustaining injury;
- a serious injury requiring surgery;
- a long, arduous rehabilitation with restriction from their preferred sports;
- a lack of pre-injury competence on return to sport;
- being replaced in their positions by team-mates.

Researchers also pointed out that for some athletes their sport provided a socially acceptable outlet for aggression. With this outlet removed, anger and depression can increase to unacceptable levels.

The writers emphasised the importance of raising awareness of this issue with coaches, athletic trainers and parents:

> Coaches, athletic trainers and parents who tell an injured athlete to 'hang in there' and 'be tough' are impairing the individual's internal and social permission to be open about stress.

> It can become very tangled when children connect their identity and personal self worth to athletics.

(Quoted in NATA 1995)

Issues for schools

- *Talented pupils need the emotional outlet provided by using their talents. For many, this may be the most important part of their lives, both inside and outside school. This needs to be recognised and respected.*
- *Many important activities for talented pupils (training sessions, rehearsals, and so on) take place on the edges of the curriculum, i.e. before or after school, in lunch hours or even – in the case of instrumental music lessons – by withdrawal from mainstream lessons. Denying a pupil access to these (e.g. as a punishment for bad behaviour or uncompleted homework in other subjects) can provoke a strong emotional response.*
- *'Single-minded . . . arrogant . . . stroppy . . . sensitive . . . highly strung . . . Only happy when practicing, rehearsing or performing . . . Constantly in trouble at school, but highly praised for his behaviour and attitude in musical groups outside school – but only if the musicians running them are of a good standard.' These are the words a parent used to describe their highly talented son! Although not all talented pupils are 'difficult', a significant minority find it hard to conform, preferring to identify with a peer group outside school, based on their talent area.*

INSET: *some case studies for discussion*

Scenario 1

Tom (a Year 9 pupil at a large rural comprehensive school) has known from an early age that he wants to be a musician. His dream is to play in a professional orchestra, and his violin lessons are the highlight of his week. The school's policy is to withdraw pupils from academic lessons on a rota basis, to avoid missing the same subject each week. Word comes from the German teacher that Tom has just walked out of her class to attend his violin lesson, despite her saying he had to miss his lesson as they were having a quiz in German that day.

(a) Was Tom justified in walking out? What other issues might emerge from this incident, e.g. with the Head of Music, or with the instrumental music teacher (who is self-employed)?

(b) As Gifted and Talented Coordinator, the Deputy Head has asked you to meet with the German teacher to explain the rationale for school policy on instrumental lessons. What arguments might you use to help her to understand Tom's point of view?

Scenario 2

Emma is eight years old and attends her local primary school. Although she has shown exceptional talent in the arts (e.g. designing and constructing a '3D theatre' for use with special lenses) in the rest of her work she is a 'walking disaster area'. She is almost wilfully untidy, and the only school equipment she consistently remembers to bring from home is her box of art pens and pencils, which are kept in immaculate order. Her relationships with other pupils are often strained, owing to her changes of mood and insistence on going her own way. As a result, she has consistently been the subject of bullying since she began school. Although academically in the 'superior' level, her achievement lags far behind her potential. Staff feel that, despite the frustrations of teaching her, she is undoubtedly a candidate for the gifted and talented register at the school. However, there is some disagreement over whether to classify her as an all-rounder or as talented in art. Some feel that as she is so unmotivated in her academic work it would be best to focus on her talent in art, offering her extra opportunities to work in various media, and to be involved in a forthcoming masterclass with a visiting artist. Others feel that the art might be used as a 'carrot' to encourage her to perform better academically. Extra opportunities in art would be offered, but only if her appalling track record in other areas were to improve.

Which approach do you feel is more likely to reduce Emma's alienation from school and improve her overall achievement?

Summary

Many of our preconceptions about talented people are based on the behaviour and attributes of a few high-profile individuals. When those with no musical training are asked to picture a 'musician', often they think of a solo violinist – perhaps even a prodigy – rather than the rank and file 'cellist who spends his entire career playing a supporting role. All eyes are on the lead singer in a pop group, but often we overlook the backing singers. We read about the exploits of David Beckham, but seldom think about the personalities and daily lives of footballers in small, non-league clubs. For every Tracey Emin in the art world, there are scores and scores of graphic designers, illustrators, and a host of others who would describe themselves as 'artists'.

The talent area as a whole, and in fact each individual area of talent, covers such a vast range of roles and personality types that it is impossible to generalise about what talented pupils are like.

Perhaps the only thing that can be said with confidence about talented individuals in the creative arts and in sport is that to a truly talented individual their area of talent is much more than just their 'favourite subject'. It is an integral part of their personality, and a vital mode of physical and emotional self-expression. In other words, to possess a talent is as much to do with what the talent means to you, as it does with your level of proficiency.

I'm often asked what it *feels like* to be talented in the arts or sport.

If you are reading this book then chances are you are passionate about teaching. It gives you a 'buzz', it is a kind of 'performing art', you can get a bit rusty over the summer holidays... all of these things point to the fact that teaching is a skill. Quite apart from the knowledge of a particular subject, the conveying of that knowledge, engaging and motivating pupils, and a whole range of other skills and personality traits characterise teaching as an art. This can give at least some of the flavour of being involved in a skills-based area.

Yet it is difficult – if not impossible – to communicate fully the feeling of identity, the total absorption, the emotional commitment, the *intensity* of devotion to one's area of talent. Most people have interests across a range of areas. They may be keen hobbyists of one sort or another, or extremely committed to some aspect of their work or profession. Yet for truly talented people, the total focus of life is on their talent area.

This is not to say that all talented pupils love to play, sing, dance, etc. In fact it is often much more of a love–hate relationship – a constant battle between their obsessive interest in their area of talent, and the constant challenge of developing sufficient skill to express themselves effectively, to win the match, to move the audience.

The legendary tennis 'great', John McEnroe, gives this description of his relationship with the sport which brought him so much success:

> Tennis, obviously, turned out to be an incredible thing for me, an amazing roller-coaster ride... but the truth is that I didn't really want to pursue it until it just pursued me.

Many athletes seem truly to love to play their sport. I don't think I ever felt that way about tennis. I looked forward to the practice and preparation, but the match itself was a constant battle for me, against two people: the other guy and myself.

(McEnroe with Kaplan 2003, p. 30)

Perhaps *fascination* is a better word for the bond between a talented person and their area of talent. John McEnroe began to play tennis at the age of eight:

From an early age I had good hand-eye coordination, and as soon as I picked up a tennis racket, there was another dimension: in a way I can't explain, I could feel the ball through the strings. From the beginning, I was fascinated by all the different ways you could hit a tennis ball – flat, topspin, slice. I loved the way a topspin lob would sail over my opponent's head, dive down just inside the baseline, then go bouncing out of his reach. I loved to take my racket back for a hard forehand or backhand, and then, at the very last millisecond, feather the ball just over the net for an angled drop-shot that would leave the other guy flat-footed and open-mouthed. I hit thousands of practice balls at the Douglaston Club backboard, testing all the possibilities...

(*ibid.*, p. 22)

The challenge of the talented pupil

To return to our opening question: What are talented pupils like? They cover the whole gamut of personality types. There are significant differences between those drawn to particular sports, particular arts and, within these, to particular roles. Those blessed with an 'artistic temperament' may prove to be difficult to handle. Talented pupils may have a love–hate relationship with their talent area.

Perhaps the greatest challenge for schools, in dealing with talented pupils, is their obsessive interest in something which is not the main aim of the school. Whether or not they are high achievers academically, developing their 'non-academic' talents is likely to be far more important to them than their academic work.

CHAPTER 9

The talent-enhancing school: characteristics and ethos

High quality and maximum participation: the talent enhancing school

We all know of schools – both primary and secondary – which have an outstanding reputation for sport or for the arts. Even before the days of Beacon Schools and Specialist Colleges, there were some schools which seemed to have a knack for producing more than their fair share of outstanding pupils in the talent realm.

These 'talent-enhancing' schools combine **high levels of participation** with **high achievement**, and display:

- an unusually large number of pupils involved in the particular activity (e.g. high numbers in extracurricular groups, and/or pursuing GCSE, GNVQ and A-level courses);

- an exceptionally high standard of achievement, e.g. success in competitions (sporting or artistic), high levels of attendance at productions and events, outstanding examination results, recognition by outside agencies for excellence (e.g. Ofsted, professional bodies, universities, etc.).

It's tempting to attribute this to the presence of an outstanding teacher or coach, or of an unusually supportive or interested parent base. Perhaps the school has an inspiring coach, or an art teacher with a reputation for motivating pupils to do their best, or a drama teacher engaged in innovative work in the field. As for catchment area, I know of a state secondary school in North London where a particularly large number of parents are creative arts professionals; hence pupils in the school might be expected to have an extra dose of home support for their work in the arts (or an extra dose of the 'artistic temperament' in their genes!).

However, this is not the only explanation for the existence of 'talent-enhancing' schools. An outstanding staff and an unusual set of parents certainly contribute to high-calibre work, but there is something of the 'chicken and egg' situation here: a charismatic music teacher might build up a good programme at a school; the good reputation for music then attracts good staff, and so on. Or a school might gain a reputation for the visual arts; with the result that parents with children with those talents are drawn to that particular school. I know of a primary school which has a thriving Jazz Band that regularly appears in the Schools' Proms at the Royal Albert Hall. If I were a musical parent living in the area, I know I would move hell and high water for my child to attend this particular school.

Good teaching is a vital element in high achievement, yet outstanding staff alone will not make for a talent-enhancing school. The outstanding teaching may be being delivered to only a few youngsters. For example, a school might have outstanding examination results for GCSE Music, yet only have a very small number of candidates.

A subtle elitism

The fact is that in some schools with a high reputation for the creative arts or sport, there is actually relatively low participation outside a core of highly able pupils. In some cases a high reputation can actually contribute to a subtle elitism, which actually militates against wider participation. It may be that the expectations are such that weaker children are discouraged from pursuing examination courses in the subject, or excluded from performing groups, which remain firmly 'audition only'. Within the classroom, this subtle elitism is reinforced; for instance, certain pupils are referred to as 'our artists' or 'our musicians', with the unspoken message being that they are a breed apart. In some schools with a high reputation for sport, the focus is entirely on the 'first team'; ruthless selection takes place early on in a pupil's school career, and only the top players receive coaching from the most able staff. While this may make for large numbers of trophies for school teams, it can have a very demotivating effect on youngsters, who may have been leading players in a less competitive pool of applicants. (It would be interesting to see how many of these students gain the confidence, skills and enthusiasm to continue with sport in later life.)

Although such schools can be very popular, achieve a 'high profile' and attract numbers of pupils whose talents are already well developed, there can still be significant wastage of ability among the other pupils.

CASE STUDY

A few years ago I was asked to take over an evening class for adult students at a college of further education in the Nottingham area. The aim of the course was to teach basic singing technique, with no prior experience required. Almost all of these students had been 'unsuccessful' in music lessons at school. Most had not participated in any musical activities at school; a few had been members of church choirs; and virtually none of them could read music. Yet they were all keen to learn how to express themselves through singing, and to be able to perform music that they liked. At the end of the second evening class, I was invited to join them for their regular post-class socialising at the nearby pub. It was fascinating to hear about the musical interests and motivation of these students, who ranged in age from 19 to nearly 60. (One had taken the class solely so he could learn how to sing his favourite Beatles' number to his wife to be!) In the class there was one student in particular with an outstanding voice. He was an Afro-Caribbean, about thirty years old, who worked as an administrator in the local council offices. The class involved quite a bit of vocal technique, and once he began working on the various exercises, a tenor voice of professional calibre emerged, with a range and quality suited to grand opera. If he had been able to read music, he would have been in demand throughout the region and beyond. (Good tenor voices are in short supply!) Although the school he attended was known locally for its music provision, I was surprised to hear that he had not been involved in any musical activities while at school: unable to read music or to play an instrument, he had felt excluded from the music programme, which offered few opportunities for those lacking these skills. He confessed that he had been disruptive and unmotivated at school, leaving with few qualifications and many regrets. The frustration is that – with a more inclusive approach in his school – he might have been encouraged to join the choir and pick up the basics of music-reading. (It really was an exceptional voice.)

The ethos of the school

An interesting perspective is provided by the experience of instrumental music teachers, who move between a number of different schools during a given week: the teacher remains the same, but the school changes. Any instrumental music teacher will tell you that there are often striking differences between the schools they visit. Some have well-motivated pupils who seldom miss lessons and usually remember to turn up on time, with their instrument and music in hand. Others are a nightmare – lessons are missed, music forgotten, instruments left behind at home. Some schools have large numbers of pupils learning an instrument; others just a few. In some schools pupils tend to carry on with their lessons for several years, moving on to the higher grades; in others they drop out after only a short time.

There are many issues relating to instrumental music provision in schools.[1] At the risk of over-simplifying a complex situation, socio-economic profile certainly plays a part: generally, in areas of high social deprivation fewer pupils are involved in instrumental tuition, and standards are lower in terms of reliable attendance at lessons and so on. However, this is not the entire explanation, for in the 'leafy suburb' schools (with a largely middle-class, affluent intake of pupils) there are also significant differences between schools, both in the number of pupils and in their motivation.

---

1   For a discussion of some of the issues involved, see the report on the Keele University Young People and Music Participation Project (funded by the Economic and Social Research Council) by Lamont *et al.* (2001).

CASE STUDY: THREE 'LEAFY SUBURB' SCHOOLS

Schools A, B and C are all comprehensive schools located in relatively affluent areas of a major city. All are heavily oversubscribed. Parents pay a premium to buy houses in the catchment areas for all three schools, which achieve some of the best examination results locally and have a reputation for good behaviour.

School A is a Catholic comprehensive school with excellent examination results and a thriving sixth form. The head teacher, staff and parents alike are keen to see the school develop its potential in music. Many of the children learn instruments privately or through the local music service, and the feeder primary schools have good choral traditions. Yet in the comprehensive, music languishes, with small examination groups, only one extracurricular group (a very lacklustre 'school orchestra'), and no sense of excitement or achievement in music lessons. The Head of Music has been there for many years. He is unenthused about his job, and is considering a career change. In this school, the whole-school and parental support is there, but it is not coupled with good provision either within or outside the curriculum.

School B is another large comprehensive, renowned locally for its academic achievements. In this school, there are several strong extracurricular groups and a reasonable level of participation. However, the school's emphasis on academic achievement means that there is constant pressure on the music department to avoid disrupting academic progress. Pupils receiving music lessons at school are not allowed to leave academic lessons, once they are in Year 10 or above, to avoid missing examination work. Instead, they can only attend their music lessons in the lunch hours or breaks. This has a knock-on effect on lower school pupils, who miss out on having lunchtime lessons. As a result many give up having lessons at all.

Note: It is often in these more 'academic' schools where music is thought of as a 'frill' (see comments in Chapter 2) or polite accomplishment, where pupils are told to prioritise academic work over practice, and where pupils regularly give up because 'my parents say I mustn't miss any more Maths (or French or Geography...) lessons to attend instrumental lessons'; with the implication that anything 'academic' must be more worthwhile. And how many academically able pupils have found it a struggle to convince their parents that taking GCSE Physical Education is not a 'waste' of a subject?

School C has large numbers of pupils involved in instrumental music lessons...in fact, every pupil learns an instrument. The head teacher is an enthusiast for music, and supports the department well, both in terms of staffing and equipment. School concerts are major – and frequent – events: so many pupils participate that it is impossible for all the performing groups to play in every concert. Performing groups regularly visit feeder primary schools, to serve as role models for younger pupils, and to ensure an enthusiastic response to the free instrumental lessons in Year 7. One girl from this school transferred to School B in Year 8 when her family moved house.

Although she did not come from a 'musical home' her parents had been delighted that she had been learning the flute at School C, using one of the school instruments. The policy in School B was to give priority for lessons and instruments to those who were coming in in Year 7. She went on a waiting list for flute lessons, but never made it to the top of the list. She has had no further involvement in music.

Elements/ingredients of a talent-enhancing school

To summarise: talent-enhancing schools couple high standards of achievement in the talent realm, with large numbers of pupils involved. Why are they so successful? By drawing from a larger base, they are likely to attract more pupils whose talents would otherwise have been unrecognised. Their success then draws in other pupils to the school.

What is it that makes for this powerful combination of inclusivity and quality? The talent-enhancing school is characterised by:

■ *A 'talent friendly' ethos* – Are systems and policies formulated with an awareness of the needs and aspirations of talented pupils, or is the emphasis solely on academic work? Are the special needs of talented pupils understood by all staff? Are measures in place to allow for sufficient flexibility in meeting these needs?

■ *Consistent and inclusive approaches to identifying talented pupils* – Is there a 'can do' approach to pupils' participation in sport and the arts, with policies that 'cast the net widely' in offering opportunities to as many pupils as possible; or is an underlying elitism in operation?

■ *Clear strategies for talent development* – Once a pupil begins to show promise in a talent area, how does the school encourage him or her to stick to it, to put in the necessary time, effort and commitment?

■ *Access to a range of provision, both within and outside the curriculum* – How are talented pupils challenged to develop their skills, within the classroom, on the sports field, in extracurricular activities and through links with the wider community?

Creating a 'talent friendly' ethos

In schools with a 'talent friendly' ethos, staff, pupils and parents are aware of the many benefits (for all pupils) which come from participation in the talent areas.

The head teacher's role

The head teacher's attitude is fundamental to the ethos of the school. Particularly in primary schools, it is hard to imagine a truly 'talent-enhancing school' existing without the support of the head teacher. In secondary schools, talent may still thrive, but at departmental level; and good staff may find lack of support 'from the top' to be so discouraging that they move on to other posts.

As for the head teacher themselves – whether primary or secondary – it is important to stress that they need *not* be 'talented' themselves. It is often assumed that it is helpful to have a head who knows something about the talent areas, and preferably has some experience of them at first hand; however in my experience it is often the heads who were not offered the opportunity to develop their talents as youngsters, who are the most enthusiastic that their pupils should benefit by receiving these opportunities. (Conversely, I know of more than one case where having an ex-Head of Music as head teacher has actually inhibited musical development, through constant interference!)

In my first Head of Department post (in an all boys' school), the head teacher wanted music to be 'the heart of the school': even though he could not participate in any musical activities himself, he attended every musical event. When the choir sang at the Royal Festival Hall, he was there, even though he had not had a single evening off from school events for several weeks past. I have a treasured collection of handwritten notes from this particular head, saying how much he and his wife had enjoyed the boys' singing, how proud he was of them, and how much he appreciated all the effort that had gone into rehearsing and arranging for musical events. He was truly a 'talent-enhancing head teacher', who also attended every major school sporting event, and helped to form and coach a rowing team at the school.

Increasing respect for the talent realm

Changing people's perceptions of whole subject areas takes time and a determined approach. The Government's current emphasis on the creative arts and sport is very welcome, but when dealing with parents and pupils, part of the challenge is to combat deep-rooted prejudices about the importance of practical/applied subjects as compared with academic/theoretical ones.[2] I was once told – by an able Year 8 pupil from a supportive, middle-class family – that his parents had told him not to include any of the 'unimportant' subjects on their list of Parents' Evening appointments: and this was in a specialist school for the Performing Arts.

Thanks to the National Qualifications Framework, pupils are now awarded UCAS points (for university admission) linked to their level of achievement in graded examinations in music and in speech and drama. This recognition of the time and commitment involved in pursuing a talent to a high level is an important first step to improving the status of the arts. Yet I wonder how many staff and parents are aware of this development? The introduction of GCSE and A-level Physical Education has also been an important first step in raising the status of sport. However, in too many cases, the rewards of sustained development in the talent areas are still undervalued by those who have never experienced them at first hand.

---

2   The history of the term 'academic' is an interesting one. Initially it simply referred to 'a school', but by the end of the twentieth century it had come to mean 'of no practical use'!

One key to improving the status of the performing arts and sport lies in increasing the participation of pupils. Once parents and pupils have experienced at first hand the benefits of high-quality involvement in the creative arts and sport, the battle is often won.

The following are some practical strategies for raising the image of the talent realm with parents, staff and pupils:

- Help raise the profile of the arts and sport by including information about goings-on in the arts and sport in assemblies and newsletters. Often pupils – and even other staff – are unaware of achievements and events in other areas of the school.

- Ensure that a member of the senior management team (preferably, the head teacher) attends school productions, concerts, art exhibitions, major sporting events. Parents (and staff) *do* notice!

- Display certificates and trophies from the full range of pupils' achievements. I know of one school – where the emphasis was on sporting achievements, to the detriment of the creative arts – which refused to display a formal photograph of a musical group in the school foyer. Despite the group having achieved national recognition, it wasn't felt suitable for display outside the department.

- Consider presenting in assemblies certificates gained in activities outside school. Seeing pupils awarded certificates for Speech and Drama, Music, Judo, Dance and so on can encourage other pupils to appreciate these achievements, and even to follow in their footsteps. (Note: this needs to be done without embarrassing the pupils involved. See the comments below, about allowing pupils to keep a 'low profile' if they wish.)

- Invite artists/coaches into the school for extended periods of time, so that other members of staff and parents alike can see the positive effects on pupils of a sustained involvement in a project.

- Encourage your creative arts and sport departments to become involved in cross-curricular projects both among themselves and with more 'academic' departments: for example, a history project linked with drama or art or music can provide a much wider perspective for pupils; a music project on musical instruments links well with practical work in design technology and/or with theoretical work on sound waves in science; dance can be linked to musical composition; and musical composition to art (perhaps inspired by the work of great artists, or by the pupils themselves). The possibilities – and the benefits for pupils – are limitless.

- Dedicate a week of school time (perhaps in the summer term) to highlight the arts and/or sport. Encourage the use of drama, music and movement in a range of lessons during the designated week, providing a list of ideas and examples to help staff from other curriculum areas to see ways in which the talent areas can enhance their teaching.

- Have staff learn an instrument for a term, alongside student 'mentors', to give them an idea of the time, effort – and enjoyment – involved in learning an instrument.

- Challenge pupils to improve their fitness by setting up an informal competition between different houses or year groups.
- Provide an 'open evening' or 'open weekend' when pupils and parents can use the facilities of the art department to sample what is on offer.
- Create an ad hoc choir for a special event, involving all of Year 7, to give them the opportunity to experience the thrill of performing.
- Use some of the INSET ideas from Chapter 3 ('The talent area: benefits for pupils') to help raise awareness of the importance of the talent realm, and of the contribution that a sustained commitment to developing his or her talent can make to a pupil's development in a whole range of areas, including self-esteem, social skills and academic achievement.

Meeting the needs of talented pupils

Systems and policies operating on a whole-school basis or within departments help to create the ethos of the school. Some schools value their academic reputation to the extent where talented pupils can suffer. Others are simply unaware of the pressures experienced by pupils with a major commitment to the creative arts or sport, on top of the usual demands of school.

CASE STUDY

I know of one very talented musician whose comprehensive school – anxious to move up in the league tables – had an inflexible rule that all pupils in the higher ability groups must take 11 subjects at GCSE. Since he was already working on graded examinations in two instruments and in singing, attending a whole range of ensembles outside school, and commuting to London weekly to attend the junior department of one of the conservatoires, his parents approached the school to see if they would allow him to reduce his subject load, and to spend some of his free periods in the music block, practising. The school refused, insisting on the 'usual' 11 subjects. At the beginning of Year 11 he fell ill with glandular fever, with disastrous results. He failed to achieve good grades in his GCSEs, nor did he achieve the 'distinction' grades he needed in his music examinations for entrance to music college. (A disastrous outcome for all concerned.)

What can a school realistically provide for its talented pupils?

Access to specialist coaching (preferably on a sustained basis) is a vital element in talent development. Yet many schools will find this problematic with at least some of the talent areas. Most primary and secondary schools will not be able to offer intensive training in classical dance, for example. Certain sports require equipment and expertise beyond the reach of many schools. Art tuition in school may be focused on graphics and design, rather than fine art (or vice versa).

However, *all* schools can help to meet the needs of their talented pupils through approaches such as those listed below:

- **Allowing them time to develop and practise their skills**, whether tuition takes place inside or outside school hours. This may involve flexibility in terms of option blocks (for example, to allow for specialism in a range of the creative arts); negotiating reduced workloads, perhaps by allowing them fewer homework or coursework commitments, and/or allowing for some flexibility in the number of GCSE and A-level subjects taken; releasing pupils from school to attend competitions and other events.

- **Recognising the commitment of pupils *and* staff involved in talent development**. A talent-enhancing school creates an atmosphere where all staff feel valued, not just those in the 'core' academic subjects. Drama staff spend enormous amounts of time working on school productions; Heads of Music Departments are often juggling a range of other activities (Associated Board Examinations, large teams of visiting instrumental/vocal teachers, as well as school concerts and public events such as Awards Evenings); PE Departments are responsible for a whole range of trips outside school, on a regular basis. Staff with heavy extracurricular commitments need to feel supported, e.g. through reduced cover commitments or a lessening of teaching load.

- **Providing an audience** for their work.

- **Involving them in ensemble/team work**, where appropriate, to develop their skills and experience.

- **Encouraging them to seek the company of their peers and the best possible coaching and training**, even if it means referral to outside agencies and groups (sports clubs, the local music service, a local college of further education art department).

- **Showing a sensitive understanding about their passionate commitment to their talent area**. Do not deny them participation in their talent area as a punishment or incentive to do coursework. All too often, talented youngsters are denied the emotional expression and release they need, by well meaning staff, trying – ill advisedly – to 'force' them to complete coursework.

> Feelings run deep, and a person's self-esteem is integrated very closely with being able to pursue his or her talent area. The footballer, David Beckham writes about a time when he was injured and could not play or train (he was aged ten at the time):
>
> > With me it was my heels: pins and needles at first and then, later, aching during and after games. I tried putting bits of foam in my boots but eventually I had to have a complete break from football. I couldn't play, I couldn't train. Couldn't even have a kickabout over at the park. That was the longest five weeks of my life and, in a way, I've never got over it. Having to watch football instead of playing it still has me climbing up walls.
>
> (Beckham with Watt 2003, p. 27)

- Recognise that **most talented pupils would much prefer being in a specialist environment** where they can do nothing but pursue activities in their talent area all day, in the company of their peers, and with the best possible coaching available! This goes far beyond the enhanced curriculum on offer in specialist colleges. For the truly talented, their devotion verges on obsession. Their strong sense of identification with their talent group might lead to extremes of dress and behaviour. Be aware that many talented pupils will never fit entirely comfortably into a 'normal' school environment.

Issues for schools

Staff may be reluctant to refer talented youngsters on to outside agencies, for fear of losing them for school teams and ensembles. The Premier League 'Football Academies', for example, do not allow their players to participate in any games which are not under the supervision of their coaching team.

There is a good reason for this: muscle memory – on which so many of the talent areas are based – is very persistent. We all know how hard it is to correct a bad habit that has been established; by keeping players completely under the supervision of their own coaching staff, the aim is to avoid the development of any bad habits. Be aware of this conflict of interest, and try to put the pupils' best interests at heart.

Note: In the performing arts, pupils who are highly committed may well be involved in outside groups (either in the community or through a County or LEA Music and Performing Arts Service). Again, the knock-on effect of this can be reduced participation in school groups, which are then perceived by pupils as being at a lower level. One way to tackle this is to negotiate some guidelines with leaders of the outside group. Many already have policies which help to support participation in school groups, e.g. by giving priority to school concerts and events. Working in partnership with outside groups is often the best way forward.

Identification and task commitment: the 'find 'em and make 'em do it' approach

One of the hallmarks of a talent-enhancing school is its commitment to using consistent and inclusive approaches to identifying talented pupils. Such schools have a 'can do' approach to pupils' participation in sport and the arts, with policies that 'cast the net widely' in offering opportunities to as many pupils as possible (see Chapter 7, 'An inclusive approach to talent-spotting').

This approach works best when coupled with a clear set of strategies for talent development. Success in the talent area requires effort, time and commitment. Whether or not schools have the expertise 'in house' to develop pupils' talents to the full, the school environment can still contribute much to the development of task commitment.

It is **task commitment** which will ultimately determine success in a talent area. Initial ability, parental support, good coaching...all will come to nought if the youngster is not dedicated, interested and enthused about the talent area. We not only have to 'find 'em' (hopefully through an inclusive approach to selection) but then we have to 'make 'em do it' (by helping them to develop the necessary task commitment).

Inclusive approaches to selection

Selection procedures are inevitably flawed. Even pupils who seem to 'have it all' in terms of potential can turn out to be quite unsuited; and some rather unlikely candidates can turn out to have the potential for success.

CASE STUDY

In the Junior Band project described in an earlier chapter, there were two boys who began learning the bassoon. One lad was in Year 8, and had been on the waiting list for bassoon lessons for over a year. He came from a musical family, had achieved Grade 5 in Piano and had large hands (an important prerequisite for bassoon playing!).

The other was a smallish Year 7 boy, who had signed up for the clarinet. When I demonstrated the bassoon to the group and asked for volunteers to learn this unusual instrument, his hand shot up. He came from an 'ordinary home' (supportive, but no one had ever learned an instrument), he did not read music and his hands wouldn't quite reach the keys!

Since we were using an inclusive approach (an open access band programme initially, with selection for individual lessons delayed until after the first two terms), we were able to include the younger boy in the band. We had two spare instruments, so we decided to let him have a go on the rather beaten-up, second-best instrument.

In the end the elder boy – who had seemed to be our brightest prospect – never 'took to' the bassoon. He found it difficult to make a really good sound, and had other musical options he enjoyed more (his piano playing) which competed for practice time. Although he attended rehearsals regularly, he struggled, and after two terms it was agreed between parents and school that he should give up the bassoon, and concentrate on his piano playing, which was progressing very well.

Meanwhile, the younger lad responded to the challenge of learning the bassoon, including the simple practical problem of carrying a large and heavy instrument back and forth to school. By Christmas, his hands had grown sufficiently to (just!) reach the keys, and he was an enthusiastic member of the junior band, determined to master whatever parts came his way. He 'got a buzz' out of playing the bassoon. Even with a very poor-quality instrument (much repaired), he was playing really well, and practised determinedly, in the small semi-detached house where his family lived.

When the older boy gave up the better instrument it was given to Mark, who improved still more. In Year 8 he began individual lessons with a bassoon teacher at school. By the end of that year he had passed his Grade 3 Bassoon examination with Merit, and by Year 9 was playing in the County Youth Orchestra. As a spin-off he also took up piano, sang in the school choir, and later on took several leading roles as a singer in school musicals. In time he attended one of the London conservatoires and played professionally, eventually ending up teaching bassoon for a large music service.

Selection takes time

Without the Junior Band experiment, Mark would never have known what a bassoon was, much less gone on to make a career of playing and teaching it! In the fullness of time, it became clear which boy had both the ability and the interest to play seriously. If we had used standard selection procedures, the older boy would have been selected to have lessons; the younger boy – with no previous musical experience and hands that wouldn't quite reach the keys – would never have been given the opportunity in the first place. After a few months, the older boy would have given up his lessons, and we would have looked for another 'likely candidate'.

This more inclusive approach in the early stages enabled Mark's talent to emerge…not overnight, but over the period of a year or so. The lad who should have done well didn't – not through lack of parental support, or poor musical background, or anything tangible; it just wasn't the right activity for him. If he had been our only bassoon candidate that year, and had received individual lessons, only to give up, the resources would have been wasted. Conversely, the usual tests and selection procedures would never have discovered and nurtured Mark's talent for playing the bassoon.

As for 'make 'em do it'…

Having emphasised the importance of choice and enthusiasm in the selection process, the key challenge is then to encourage pupils to sustain that initial enthusiasm. One reason that pupils from 'musical', 'artistic' and 'sporting' homes do well in the talent areas is because their families understand and encourage the task commitment involved in developing talents to the full. They insist they do their practice, ensure that they attend training sessions, enter them for competitions and exhibitions.

The tennis player, John McEnroe put it like this:

I guess I would correlate my story to those you hear about kids learning to play the piano. Every now and then, someone says, 'I just loved to play six hours a day.' But mostly they say, 'God, my parents forced me to play, they forced me to take those lessons; but I'm sure glad they made me do it.'…Look at almost any of the great players. Would they have succeeded anyway if they hadn't been pushed?…I had dinner with Richard Williams [father of Venus and Serena Williams]…and he told me, 'Kids have no idea what they want to do most of the time…Look, I picked something great for them, something that'll give them a tremendous living and a tremendous life. It's crazy to think that they were capable of making that decision when they were young. So of course I pushed them, but they needed to be pushed.'

McEnroe goes on to say:

And so my parents pushed me...they were the driving force...I seriously doubt if I would've been the player I became if I hadn't been forced into it in some way.

(McEnroe with Kaplan 2003, p. 30)

In loco parentis

While school can never replace the support provided by a sporting, artistic or musical home, it can certainly contribute to 'making 'em do it'. School structures and systems can foster task commitment or, conversely, can undermine it, producing the 'prima donna effect' – where pupils are rewarded with attention, status and performing/ playing opportunities, without 'earning' them through regular attendance and commitment (see also p. 108).

Some strategies for developing task commitment

- Have clear expectations about participation in extracurricular groups. How will pupils be selected for leading roles, places on the team, membership of certain groups, solo work in concerts, public displays of art work, and so on. This also helps to ensure progression, since pupils can then set themselves realistic, attainable goals, e.g. to have artwork exhibited in the classroom, then in the entrance hall, then on the school's website.

- Take attendance regularly at extracurricular activities. This can be done formally, by 'calling the register', or informally, by leaving registers out for pupils to sign.

- Follow up on pupils who have attended for a time, but then dropped out. Without pressuring them gently try to find out why they have lost interest, and invite them to return.

- Give pupils an option of a 'taster' fortnight (or half-term or term, if more appropriate to the activity), after which they need to make a commitment to the group or activity for a given period (a term, until the next concert, until the school production in the spring, and so on). If commitment and attendance at out-of-school activities are problematic in your school, send a note home for parents to sign. That way they will be aware of what is involved and will share and support the goals of the group as they work towards, for example, an event or competition.

- Encourage responsibility and raise pupils' awareness of their commitments by using a simple self-reporting form for absences (see Figure 9.1). It can also be useful in drawing attention to clashes with other departments' activities (e.g. revision sessions, extra rehearsals or training sessions and so on). Pupils –

particularly all-rounders – can find themselves in the midst of a battleground of competing demands. If potential conflicts are spotted early on, staff can then negotiate for pupils' time; this helps to avoid placing pupils under too much pressure.

■ Set goals for groups. The challenge of working towards a goal can help to motivate pupils, both to attend and to give of their best. This is particularly important in the talent areas, where self-expression is so important. Competitions, festivals (both competitive and non-competitive), 'friendly' matches... even a simple visit to a local primary school or nursing home can contribute to team spirit and help to create the momentum which encourages task commitment.

■ Avoid giving leading roles, places in the team, solos in the concert, etc., to those who are not setting a good example in terms of learning their lines, turning up for practice, helping others to develop. You will not be doing them any favours by doing so, since once they are outside the 'small pond' of their school, they will be passed over in favour of youngsters who are easier to work with, and more reliable.

Music Department

Absence Report Form

Name _____ Form_____

Extracurricular group _____

Day and date of absence _____

Reason for absence (be precise) _____

_____

_____

_____

This is my: first   second   third   absence this term.
(circle one)

Signed: _____

Figure 9.1 Sample form used for self-reporting of absences in extracurricular groups

Avoiding the 'prima donna effect'

Despite his celebrity off the pitch, footballer David Beckham has always been a good team player. He attributes this to his early training in a team for eight- and nine-year-olds, Ridgeway Rovers, where he learned at first hand about task commitment and the need to work together as a team:

> One important rule was that if you didn't turn up for training in the week, then you didn't play at the weekend; it was as simple as that. It was a good habit to learn… Ridgeway Rovers went about things the right way. With so many boys' sides, you notice the most talented players. They make a big fuss of the individuals in the team. That wasn't allowed with Ridgeway: any showing off and you'd be brought back down. It was all about the team. In no time, we were starting to win games ten and eleven-nil and people could see there was something special about us.
>
> (Beckham with Watt 2003, p. 26)

Providing a 'haven' for talented pupils

Good parents provide safe places where their offspring can meet together with like-minded friends, with common interests in their area of talent. The Beatles practised for hours in the converted cellar of a friend's home. The friend's parents had allowed the teenagers to make the area 'their own' and invite friends and neighbours to hear them play; and they were able to spend hours rehearsing and developing their performances.

Talent enhancing schools know that a talented pupil needs to interact with his or her peers. Making the music room, art room or drama room a 'haven' for pupils with interests in these areas can be a very valuable element in making talented pupils feel at home in what sometimes feels like an alien environment. Such a haven need not be selective – far from it. All who are actually *using* the facilities should be welcome, whatever their age or level of ability. ('Just hanging out' with friends in a convenient practice room is not appropriate: some purposeful work in the talent area is a prerequisite for 'dropping in'.) Pupils with limited access to specialised sports equipment will value the chance to use it in school (provided there is appropriate care taken with health and safety issues). Senior pupils can be helpful in adding extra supervision and mentoring for lunchtime and after-school 'drop in' activities. This helps to reinforce their identification with the talent area, and to develop a sense of responsibility.

Issues for schools
Schools can do much to create an environment in which talent will flourish:

- *Employ a range of methods to provide opportunities for pupils to show their talents over a period of time.*
- *Once talented pupils are identified, a major part of the school's role is to be* in loco parentis, *and 'make 'em do it', by encouraging task commitment and avoiding the 'prima donna effect'.*

- *Consider how access to equipment and facilities is managed at breaks, lunchtimes and after school. They could provide a valuable meeting – and working – place for talented pupils. (Try to keep access as inclusive as possible: pupils will 'self select', and some talent may emerge unexpectedly.)*

> **INSET**
>
> - Schools can often inadvertently undermine task commitment and send the wrong 'messages' to pupils about the importance of hard work in developing their talents. Working with colleagues, systematically look at how your department handles issues such as entry to 'elite' groups, attendance at training sessions and rehearsals, selection for high-profile events. Are there ways in which systems might be improved, to encourage and reinforce task commitment?
> - To what extent does your subject department stand '*in loco parentis*' to talented pupils? Is there an area within the department where pupils with similar interests can congregate during breaks and lunch hours? Are departmental facilities, e.g. the art room, available for use at these times? How might supervision be arranged (e.g. with the help of senior pupils, or ancillary staff) to allow safe access to equipment not available in pupils' homes?

The talent-enhancing school: monitoring and evaluation

The talent realm offers particular challenges in terms of the monitoring and evaluation of pupil progress. In many cases some of the most worthwhile development takes place completely outside the curriculum: in extracurricular groups, teams, and activities; and in a whole range of private tuition, from lessons in tabla, to a summer course in pottery, to serious training in judo at the local school of martial arts.

Checklists

Checklists for identification

It is common practice to use able pupil checklists to help identify and track the performance of able pupils in schools. While these can be useful in a range of academic subjects, these tend to be less useful as a means of evaluating pupils' potential in the talent areas, and in tracking their progress. Often pupils' progress in talent development does not fit comfortably into the National Curriculum requirements for particular non-academic subjects, e.g. a pupil might be in an outstanding pianist, with performance skills well in advance of his or her years, yet have considerable weaknesses in National Curriculum areas such as composition or listening and appraising. Or a pupil might be outstanding in dance, in a school where dance is not a significant part of the physical education or creative arts curriculum. A young artist may have devoted themselves so much to one style of art that their overall performance, when measured against the art and design curriculum, may not appear outstanding at all. In fact one characteristic of highly able pupils is their tendency to focus with intense devotion on one particular area, making it a challenge to encourage them to develop the necessary breadth.

Another shortcoming of identification checklists is their tendency to use language which is very vague, and hence difficult to interpret and apply. For example, one commonly-used Able Pupil Checklist for Music Departments uses terms such as 'natural understanding of musical concepts', with no examples or explanation of what this might mean in practice. The same checklist also includes 'works and communicates well in a group'. However I know one 11-year-old boy who is an excellent musician (a pianist with performing skills far beyond his years), yet has been identified by the Special Needs department at his secondary school as 'in need of very careful handling', as he refuses to work with others and is given to serious outbursts of temper.

Record sheets and National Curriculum levels

Similar issues can arise when using National Curriculum-based record sheets for tracking pupil progress, i.e. these are unlikely to provide a real sense of progress being achieved outside school, or in activities outside the curriculum. National Curriculum levels can also be misleading, since they are to a great extent counsels of perfection, i.e. what the 'ideal' student should be achieving. Take for example the Level Descriptions for Art & Design. They show progression in three main areas:

1. Exploring and developing ideas
2. Investigating and making art, craft and design
3. Evaluating and developing work.

A highly talented artist might well be so focused on their own self-expression (through 'exploring and developing ideas') as to be positively antagonistic to 'evaluating and developing work'. For example, the Level 3 Descriptions refer to pupils' need to 'comment on similarities and differences between their own and others' work, and adapt an improve their own'. Yet those who have worked with talented young artists know that they can be very stubborn about the process of commenting on and evaluating their own and others' work. Similarly, to achieve Level 8, pupils are expected to 'explore ideas and evaluate relevant visual and other information, analysing how codes and conventions are used to represent ideas, beliefs and values in different genres, styles and traditions'. It is hard to imagine some of the recent Turner Prize winners willingly engaging in this type of analysis (even though we might feel it would be 'good' for them!). National Curriculum levels are much more likely to track progression in able young artists, rather than in outstanding ones. Winner and Martino (2000, pp. 106–7) reported that, 'None of the sculptors studied...had anything good to say about their elementary or high school art classes...family and community appear more important than schools in the development of artistic ability. Not surprisingly, then, [artistically] gifted children often make their best, most inventive work out of school.'

Twice-yearly self-reporting

It is therefore vital to devise and develop effective methods to help track and support progression which takes place largely outside the curriculum.

One useful method involves self-reporting. Pupils on the gifted and talented register are asked to complete a **Talent Development: Self-reporting Form** (see page 113 for an example of such a form), on a twice-yearly basis (January and July are good times for this exercise). Self-reporting has several advantages: the school's Gifted and Talented Coordinator and the pupil's form and/or subject teacher are unlikely to have the expertise necessary to 'ask the right questions' of pupils. Many pupils will be progressing systematically through 'levels' of external examinations; these can be administered by national bodies, or by, for example, local music services (many of which have their own examination systems, especially at the lower grades). How many of us are really familiar with the details of examination levels in Speech & Drama, or in Dance? The best source of information on this is the pupils themselves.

An added benefit is the stimulus it gives to pupil self-evaluation. The process of reporting their progress on a regular basis can help pupils (especially those in the grip of 'pushy parents'!) to begin to take responsibility for their own development. It is also useful to see the 'big picture' of what is going on with talented pupils as a whole, throughout the school, not just in the discrete areas of Music, Art, Drama, Dance and Sport. Copies can be shared with the relevant subject departments (if pupils wish this). This also helps to spot all-rounders, and identify potential problems with pupils being over-committed with activities. (One important role the school can fulfil is in helping talented pupils to achieve some sense of balance in their lives.)

Note: younger pupils may need the help of a teacher or classroom assistant to complete the form.

The talent-enhancing school: provision within and outside the curriculum

Provision within the curriculum

The talent areas to some extent sit uneasily within the curriculum (see comments above). Youngsters who excel at a sport or in one of the creative arts may well be doing the bulk of their artistic and sporting activities either outside of curriculum time, or outside the school altogether. Their particular area of interest may well not even be part of the school curriculum at all. In other cases (e.g. a very talented violinist) the school curriculum does not address their particular performing skills. However all of these pupils will be receiving some statutory curriculum time in PE, Art and Design, Drama and Music.

Differentiation and extension

Stretching highly talented pupils within the classroom and on the playing field is sometimes very difficult. Using them as mentors and examples can actually backfire by arousing other pupils' jealousy and resentment. Giving them special privileges, such as allowing them to go off to use practice rooms unsupervised because they are 'musicians' can have the same effect. Many with talents being developed outside school will not want other pupils to know. Some will be under tremendous pressure from home to develop their talents, and may rebel against this pressure by refusing to co-operate in class. Others will show lots of as yet undeveloped potential, and will need drawing out to develop the confidence to succeed.

Talent Development: Self-reporting Form

[Note: if a pupil is involved in more than one talent area, please complete one form for each area.]

Name _____

Form _____ Date _____ Age _____

Talent area:

- Music (instrument/s played, singing, composing) _____
  _____

- Art & Design (particular areas of interest, e.g. pottery, graphic design, etc.) _____
  _____

- Drama_____
  _____

- Dance (give type, e.g. Irish dancing, ballet, modern, etc.) _____
  _____

- Sport (list main sport/s pursued on a regular basis, in a committed way) _____
  _____

Activities in this talent area which are pursued in school, either within the curriculum or in extracurricular groups (e.g. groups, teams, workshops, clubs and activities sponsored by the school)

Activities outside school (e.g. community groups, sports clubs, formal lessons/classes)

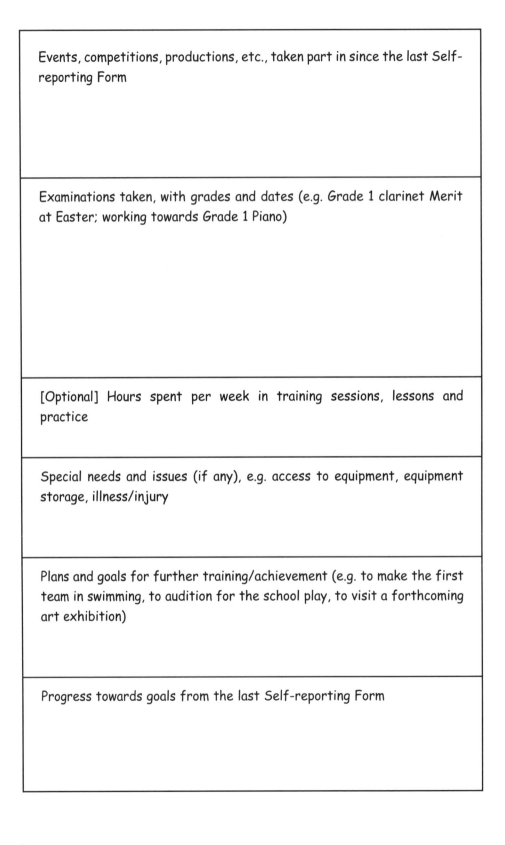

Events, competitions, productions, etc., taken part in since the last Self-reporting Form

Examinations taken, with grades and dates (e.g. Grade 1 clarinet Merit at Easter; working towards Grade 1 Piano)

[Optional] Hours spent per week in training sessions, lessons and practice

Special needs and issues (if any), e.g. access to equipment, equipment storage, illness/injury

Plans and goals for further training/achievement (e.g. to make the first team in swimming, to audition for the school play, to visit a forthcoming art exhibition)

Progress towards goals from the last Self-reporting Form

Extension tasks are likely to be more effective if they address additional *depth*, rather than additional material. In music and in art and design, for example, where differentiation in creative tasks is primarily by outcome, pupils can be set the same overall project as less able pupils, yet be challenged, for example by having them create their own 'raw materials' for (either visual or musical) composition, by encouraging them to develop their work further, or by guiding them to choose a particularly difficult subject or style. In group work in drama, and in music and dance, a natural differentiation can occur with the range of roles available. I have found that spreading able pupils between various groups works more effectively for the class as a whole, and also helps those with higher skill levels to develop social and leadership skills. Also, in my experience of classroom music teaching, placing all of the capable instrumentalists in one group can produce good results, but can demoralise the other groups. (Extracurricular groups provide an opportunity for able pupils to work with their peers, irrespective of age.) ICT can be a useful motivator for pupils who relish the practical side of their talent area, but are reluctant to engage with the more theoretical and 'academic' side of things: for example, using the web to look up 'jazz greats', or the works of well-known artists can stimulate interest. More able pupils can be challenged to search more widely, define style periods working from first principles and observation/listening, experiment with different media, and other strategies to capture their imagination.

One approach is to see the curriculum as complementing training taking place outside the school. For example, in music, pupils who are having instrumental lessons will probably already be familiar with basic musical notation and music theory; if the school curriculum focuses overly much on music theory, then the able pupils will be bored, and the others disaffected. If the focus is instead on all the pupils learning about musical styles, improvising, learning to 'busk' chords and other areas which are not so commonly covered in instrumental lessons, then a 'level playing field' can be created in the classroom, with benefits for all pupils. (Pupils who are able academically, but not 'talented' musically will also find this refreshing, since it gives them the opportunity to achieve well.)

Talented pupils are often extremely focused on their one area of interest: one particular sport rather than a range of sports, singing rather than playing an instrument, digital artwork rather than painting, and so on. This means that perhaps one of the greatest challenges in dealing with talented pupils within the curriculum is encouraging breadth of development. Every aspect of the school's curriculum needs to be seen as having potential to contribute to the development of a talented pupil. This means that expectations need to be high: that the pupils must give of their best at all times. Work within the curriculum must not be perceived by the pupil as 'marking time' or – at worst – a 'waste of time'. Even simple manoeuvres can be opportunities for improving skills or stamina in the pupil's 'main sport'. Having to explore different artistic media can actually enhance the pupil's main area of interest when they return to it. Simple classroom performances in music or drama can be done with attention to detail and a professional approach.

Resources

The range of resources for working with talented pupils within the curriculum is expanding rapidly.

The **Key Stage 3 Strategy** includes practical subject-based materials for working with gifted and talented pupils. Downloadable files can be found at: www.standards.dfes.gov.uk/keystage3/respubl/agt (correct as of June 2004). The new **Primary Strategy** promises detailed subject-specific guidance which should be of particular use to non-specialist teachers whose responsibilities include the creative arts and sport. Detailed information on provision for gifted and talented pupils (including the creative arts and sport) is contained in *Curriculum Provision for the Gifted and Talented in the Secondary School* (Eyre and Lowe 2002).

Outside the curriculum

Provision outside the school is likely to include:

- one-off events and masterclasses;
- Summer schools;
- regular out-of-school activities;
- a whole gamut of groups, lessons and courses to be found outside the school.

In the performing arts and sport, extracurricular groups are excellent places for talented pupils to enjoy the company of their peers, develop their skills to a higher level, gain performing experience, and be challenged to give of their best. Art and design students also need opportunities to display their work, to develop art and design work in response to specific demands (e.g. by working with other subject departments to produce publicity materials or the school prospectus) and to collaborate with the other creative arts (e.g. by creating scenery for the school production, or the cover for the school concert programme).

In schools that are known for their achievements in sport and in the creative arts, extracurricular groups are run on a professional basis. Rehearsals and practice/training sessions are prepared in line with an overall plan, and with progression in mind. Senior pupils are encouraged to gain experience of organising and coaching groups of younger pupils; they are supported in this by systematic training and supervision, to ensure the best possible provision for all of the pupils involved.

Talent-enhancing schools recognise the time, preparation and effort staff put into extracurricular groups, and the extent to which these are an essential part of provision for Music, Art, Dance, Drama and PE within the school. Ofsted inspections also recognise the importance of extracurricular groups, and they regularly praise the level of participation and the standards achieved. They are not seen as a 'frill' or distraction from the academic 'business' of the school, and staff are given the necessary respect, support and time to do a professional job. Pupils who take part learn valuable lessons in task commitment. (See suggestions above, p. 106.)

Primary and secondary school provision for talented pupils

In general the main challenge for primary schools is to offer as many opportunities as possible for their pupils to experience the talent areas at first hand. School productions, instrumental lessons, sporting events (with an emphasis at this stage on the FUNdamentals – see p. 52) can all make a contribution to stimulating pupils' interest. With the visual arts, school trips (whether real or 'virtual') can inspire and motivate.

Issues for primary schools

Lack of specialist teaching in the creative arts and sport is not a new problem for primary schools. The Plowden Report *Children and their Primary Schools* (DES 1967) lamented the very same thing. This means that many talented pupils – especially those whose home backgrounds do not include significant experience of sport or the creative arts – will not experience specialist tuition until secondary school. By this time, poor habits may already be ingrained, and hamper progress. Current government initiatives are attempting to address these issues. However, in the meantime an increasing number of materials and schemes of work are becoming available to ensure well planned and delivered lessons, with clear skills progression. Primary schools might also consider working in partnership with parents and with clubs and societies in their locality, to provide at least occasional 'expert' input for pupils. Artist in residence schemes, holiday sporting activities and a range of other opportunities typify the talent-enhancing primary school. Sustained provision from expert coaches and teachers is the ideal; however, much can be achieved through offering pupils a range of experiences in the talent realm.

Issues for secondary schools

By secondary school it is still not too late to discover budding talent (see Chapter 6 'Late developers and all-rounders'). In many cases the challenge will be to provide tuition and support at an appropriate level, across an ever-increasing range of activities. In many cases suitable tuition will not be within the power of the school to provide. This means that referral to outside agencies, e.g. the local music service, or local sporting clubs, may be the best solution for the child's overall development. In music, for example, the school orchestra may be very small, and operating at a very low level in terms of musical challenge. Encouraging a talented pupil to perhaps conduct the group (with support from staff) may be one solution; but it does not solve the problem of stretching the pupil to develop his or her skills as an instrumentalist. In such cases, referral to local music service groups is often the answer.

However this open-hearted support of pupils' best interests can also prove problematic. Talented young footballers who participate in Football Academies linked to Premier League clubs are actually prohibited from taking part in school sport. This is because muscle memory is such that bad habits (and weak game strategies) quickly become entrenched; so the coaches want to keep a watchful eye on their young players. From the school's point of view, it takes a degree of altruism to encourage one's best players to sign up elsewhere.

It is also important that young people move on to new challenges at a time that is right for their long-term development. Here is David Beckham – speaking again about the Ridgeway Rovers team which he felt had been so influential in his development as a player:

> Professional clubs started watching our players, and I think West Ham asked about me when I was eleven. But [the coaches]…and my dad had decided there should be no need for any of us to be involved with clubs until we were older. If you were training with a professional club the rule was you couldn't be training with a Sunday League team at the same time. I knew I didn't want that, I wasn't ready for it. We all stuck with Ridgeway. I think, in the long run, those rules [about task commitment, see quotation above, p. 108] were why so many of us went on to make a success of ourselves. We learnt about commitment and dedication right from the start.
>
> (Beckham with Watt 2003, p. 26)

Individuals vary in their readiness to move on to more advanced tuition. Some will prefer to stay with one teacher or coach, as they have a particular rapport. Others will need a change of approach at some point. Some will be ready for the extra challenges earlier than others. A pupil of mine who gained entry to a youth orchestra while only in Year 8 found that he did not fit in socially and came to dislike attending. After a period of time playing in a more junior group, he rejoined the youth orchestra in Year 10, going on to become Principal Bassoon.

Each case needs to be handled sensitively and decided on its own merits, in consultation with parents, and always with the youngster's well-being at the centre of the process.

In practice most outside agencies and groups are keen to support school activities. Many have policies which give preference to pupils' school commitments (e.g. if there is a clash of dates for a competition or performance), since it is in the best interests of all involved if schools continue to refer their most talented students. Working in partnership is the key.

Transition from primary to secondary

Transition from primary to secondary school is a sensitive time for every pupil. In the talent area there are added issues: Where will I leave my instrument case? How can I find out when my lesson is? Where is the music block? Will I be teased for carrying a violin case to school? Will I make the team? I had the lead in the primary school production in the summer…will I ever have a leading role again? Will the new art teacher like my work? How can I keep anyone from finding out I do ballet outside school?

These issues require careful handling. It is very easy to start off on the wrong foot.

For example, beware of welcoming Year 7 by asking for a show of hands as to who learned an instrument in primary school! This can intimidate those who did not have the opportunity to do so (or who began an instrument and found it was 'not for them'), and embarrass those who did.

A balance is needed, between nurturing pupils who are already on the road to developing expertise, and emphasising that it is not too late for others to be classed as artists, dancers, actors, musicians and sports men and women.

Practical help for transition

In music, pupils often give up learning an instrument in the early years of secondary school. Secondary schools can do much to support pupils. Simple steps such as making sure pupils know where to store instruments on lesson days, and instituting mentoring arrangements for older pupils to escort younger ones to the music block can make a huge difference. Often, music lessons take place in areas which are hard to find, or are even across the playing field! It is unreasonable to expect Year 7 pupils to carry heavy instruments around to lessons all day (and risk teasing from jealous or uninformed classmates) and then to find their way through a maze of practice rooms to the relevant teacher.

In sport, again be aware that pupils who were 'big fish' in the 'small ponds' of their primary schools will be feeling very uneasy on arrival. By avoiding labelling pupils as 'sporty' or not, the strengths of all pupils can gradually show themselves. It can be particularly demoralising to find that immediate entry to a school team is not possible, owing to competition. Support inclusivity by making sure pupils who have not been selected have viable and respected alternatives (e.g. form teams, after-school and lunchtime 'leagues' and so on); and make clear to all that there are opportunities for progressing to the school team in due course. Consider allowing an 'open training' approach to test and develop task commitment and allow really keen youngsters to train with the team (see the case study about water polo, Chapter 7, p. 77).

In drama, make sure there are performance opportunities for large numbers of Year 7 pupils, perhaps in their year group assemblies. Remember that many will have taken leading roles in their primary school productions, and will be keen to continue to develop their skills.

Conclusions: talented pupils in ordinary schools

The special needs of the talented

In the Preface to her important book, *Able Children in Ordinary Schools*, Deborah Eyre points out that most pupils of high ability, whether in academic areas or in the talent realm, are being educated in 'ordinary' schools (1997, pp. v–vi). In the case of the talent area, we can extend that to 'ordinary' drama groups, 'ordinary' school choirs, and in 'ordinary' local dance schools, 'ordinary' sports clubs. Truly specialist schools – where the curriculum is focused almost exclusively on the arts or sport – are extremely rare. (The UK Government's Music and Dance Scheme, which provides places for pupils to study music at specialist boarding schools, accommodates only around 800 pupils; and, for a variety of reasons, many parents will not want their children to leave home, or will not be able to afford the matching fees required for the subsidised places.) The creation of a network of specialist schools (co-ordinated by the Specialist Schools Trust) is an important first step towards trying to provide local centres of excellence for talented pupils; however, many youngsters will continue to attend schools which do not specialise in their particular area of talent. Overall, this means that 'ordinary' schools will continue to have a vital role to play in supporting and encouraging pupils to discover and develop their talents.

Time, task commitment and understanding

Since much specialised tuition in the creative arts and sport takes place outside the curriculum (and often outside the school itself), the most valuable and universal role for the talent-enhancing school will be in providing systems and opportunities for pupils to develop the task commitment to ensure success. Ideally, schools will also strive to offer flexibility (e.g. in terms of homework and other demands of the curriculum) to allow time for practice and training, and will also offer a sensitive awareness of the pressures experienced by talented pupils (including all-rounders).

In an educational climate which is coming to recognise the need for creativity and for breadth in the curriculum, there is an increasing awareness of the value of the talent realm in pupils' development. Current concerns about health and obesity among primary and secondary school pupils are also contributing to an increased interest in the role of sport and physical education in our schools. After a long period of emphasis on academic achievement, the time is ripe for re-evaluating (and revaluing) the role and status of the creative arts and sport within schools, not only in specialist schools dedicated to a particular talent area, but in all primary and secondary schools

Issues for schools
Creating a talent-enhancing school is within the reach of every primary and secondary school. By raising awareness of the benefits of the talent area, ensuring an inclusive environment for discovering talent, and focusing on high standards and task commitment, all schools have the potential to become talent enhancing. The emphasis on teamwork, high standards and the avoidance of the 'prima donna effect' will help all pupils to thrive, including those whose talent will prove to be exceptional – a 'win-win' situation for all concerned.

As a first step, audit current provision in your school, using the Talent Audit in Appendix A. Ensure that your departmental and whole-school policies for talented pupils reflect a 'talent-enhancing' approach. (For advice on writing policies for both primary and secondary schools, see Appendix D.)

Conclusion: inclusivity and quality

Inclusivity and quality

Here in the UK a long tradition of selection and privilege has tended to concentrate excellence in a small number of institutions, and within certain social groups. As a result many still associate high quality with a kind of elitism. Conversely, in some circles, the term 'inclusive' has come to mean participation at the expense of quality. As long as everyone seems to be 'having a good time' and 'expressing themselves' we feel we have achieved our aim of involving a wider group. In some cases this has resulted in criticism of certain subject areas, for not providing sufficient challenge within the curriculum.

In the arts, we sometimes mistakenly feel that pupils will be satisfied with low standards – that somehow they do not recognise high-quality work, or that they do not realise when a performance or composition or work of art is of poor quality. In my experience as a music teacher, I have found that most pupils (living as they are in an environment filled with professionally produced music) are in fact highly critical of themselves and their own efforts at music-making. Hollow praise, whether from teachers or parents, is seen for what it is. Self-expression is not enough; we need to teach the necessary skills which *enable* that self-expression – within an art form, on the football pitch, in the performance or competition.

In sport, the inevitable competition, ranking of players and the simple discipline of winning and losing mean that issues of quality are less easily side-stepped. The danger here is that steady development of technique over the long term might be sacrificed in the interests of winning in the short term. In sport, therefore, the issue becomes: what is the 'big picture' of this youngster's development in this sport over the long term? Again, how can the skills and attitude needed for success be instilled and reinforced?

Nature versus nurture

Preconceptions about the nature of talent also colour our approach to discovering and developing talent. The idea that certain individuals are blessed, genetically, with talent in the arts or in sport; that these skills only 'run in families'; that they will inevitably show themselves without having to be drawn out, are all counter-productive. We are all the products of both nature *and* nurture. We are not doing youngsters any favours by imagining that talent is solely innate – that somehow they have been given a 'gift' which, once 'discovered', doesn't need any further development. Think back to Sylvie Guillem's comments, at the end of Chapter 2, about the importance of using the 'ingredients' (i.e. of one's innate talent) well: '...it's also difficult when you have [a] gift – to know that you have to work to understand it...If you don't use them [the ingredients/talents] well, you have not a good cake or not a good something to eat.' Nor is it constructive for youngsters to think that if things do not come easily to them, it means they are not truly talented.

Talented people

Even though we cannot always provide opportunities and training for our talented pupils beyond a certain point, as schools we can still do much to reinforce the kinds of character traits which contribute to high achievement. In terms of developing talent, perhaps the greatest gift we can give our pupils is an understanding of the task commitment needed to succeed, not only in the talent areas but in any walk of life. Passionate – almost obsessive – devotion to the talent area, coupled with high standards, characterises high achievement in the talent realm.

- The ballet dancer Mikhail Baryshnikov once said, 'Working is living to me.' Now aged 56, he is still touring, as both a dancer and choreographer.

- The cellist Jacqueline du Pré, whose career was tragically ended by multiple sclerosis, continued to play in an amateur orchestra until the progress of the disease prevented her from lifting the bow.

- Despite his comments on not 'loving to play tennis', John McEnroe (now in his fifties) has brought new life and glamour to 'Seniors Tennis'.

- The artist Lucien Freud is still painting, in his eighties, and his work has recently been described as 'more modern than Tracey Emin's'.

- Although gradually moving away from theatrical roles to television and film as he found it more difficult to memorise his lines, actor John Gielgud worked as an actor to the very end. His last film role, as the Protagonist in Samuel Beckett's *Catastrophe* (directed by David Mamet; Beckett on Film DVD set, 2002) was in 2000 – the year in which he died, aged 96.

Talented people *have* to act, play, sing, paint, dance...it has become part of their soul. In my view it is this passionate, almost obsessive, attachment to one's area of talent which characterises the truly talented. We may have to 'find 'em and make 'em do it', but once they reach a certain level the momentum for success will be there. Recognising and supporting this passionate devotion with sensitivity and understanding is the key.

An inclusive approach

Elitism and early selection are *not* the prerequisites for high quality. A truly inclusive approach in fact results in higher quality, since the pool of talent is wider, broader and deeper.

An inclusive approach to discovering talent does not simply consist of a few taster sessions – an instant fix, where everyone seems to enjoy themselves, and individuals briefly become enthusiastic (perhaps in a very unrealistic way) about the possibility of dancing professionally, performing in a rock band, acting on the London stage, playing for Manchester United, competing in the Olympics. It is about *high-quality provision, wider opportunities to develop skills on a sustained basis*, and *patience* in waiting to see the fruits of this skills development over the long term.

Living as we do in an environment which values the academic over the practical, the challenge for schools is to create an environment where talent can flourish. How we deal with our preconceptions about the talent realm – and our views on the concept of 'innate ability' in general – has the potential to transform our perspective on the education of all our pupils, whatever their gifts and talents.

Auditing talent provision

Whole-school audits can take a number of forms:

- A systematic, formal audit, conducted by the Senior Management Team of a school is likely to emphasise facts and figures:
  - How many pupils are involved in the activities on offer in PE, Art & Design, Music or Drama? (Beware of counting the same pupils twice when you try to reach an overall total: in many departments there is a small core of dedicated pupils who participate in a number of groups. It is useful to know how many *different* pupils are involved, overall.)
  - How large are examination groups in the subject? How do results compare with those in other departments in the talent realm? With those in the school as a whole?
  - Are there any other indications of quality, e.g. results for pupils taking external examinations in drama or music; invitations for school groups and individuals to perform in the wider community; individual and team successes in sporting competitions; and commendations for participation in arts events and festivals can all be an indication of quality.
- Less formal audits, such as those which can be used for a whole-school INSET day, serve a different purpose. The aim here is to raise awareness and encourage self-evaluation and reflection, not to put current provision under a magnifying glass.

The audit presented here is one which has proven successful in stimulating discussion and debate in workshops and INSET days.

Ideally its use should follow a presentation of some of the issues (perhaps based on some of the INSET materials in the various chapters of this book), including some discussion and exploration of staff preconceptions about the nature of the talent (e.g. that it is mostly innate, that it is in some sense 'testable' in the same way as IQ, and so on).

The following (photocopiable documents) can then be used in small groups or pairs, as a stimulus for discussions about talent identification and development. I usually provide two versions of the pro forma – one with section titles and questions, the other with just the titles – for use as a note-taking device.

Talent Audit

Inclusivity versus elitism

- Is there open access to at least one team/performing group/activity for all pupils?
- Are auditions/try outs really necessary? When and why?
- What occasional workshops/projects are available to pupils in your school? What follow-up is there, or do these remain 'one-off' opportunities?
- Are there gender issues to be addressed in your school (e.g. for girls in sport or boys in music/dance)?

Practical issues

TIME

- How does your school deal with pupils who are pursuing a demanding schedule of practice outside school hours?
- Should schools 'make allowances', or not?
- How would you deal with the needs of a talented swimmer? A young musician? A boy who is spending many hours practising computer games? Are these activities really different, or are the issues the same?
- How do you make staff aware of pupils' other commitments?
- Is there any flexibility in the curriculum and timetable to allow pupils to pursue fewer subjects, to enable them to focus on their talent? What would the implications of this be for other pupils – and for the pupil him/her self?

TRAINING

- What mechanisms are there in your school for recommending pupils for further training and tuition outside school?
- Do you feel these are effective?
- Are staff sometimes reluctant to do this? If so, why – and what measures could be taken to address this issue (e.g. perhaps a school ruling that pupils in Music Service groups also have to participate in at least one school group)?
- What about funding?

EQUIPMENT/RESOURCES

Does your school's G&T (or other) budget allow for helping pupils with any of the following:

- subscriptions for sports clubs;

- special equipment (e.g. the purchase of running kit, the hire of a musical instrument);
- extra art/design & technology materials;
- fees for summer schools in specialist areas?

Is this an area which might be developed? Or is this outside the remit of schools?

Meeting the individual needs of talented pupils

- What strategies do you use to identify pupils whose talents are being developed outside school? How do you use this information?
- Since talented pupils have a wide variety of characteristics, is this variety reflected in the expectations of your colleagues and the ethos of the school? (For example, expecting that a 'musically talented' pupil will be good at singing and/or leading the group may cause the talents of those who prefer a supporting role to be overlooked.)
- Are teachers in your school aware of the pressures talented pupils sometimes experience, e.g. from parental expectations, from external examinations and competitions, or from worries about fitness and injury?
- Is the school sensitive to pupils' worries about performing for their peers? (Shyness does not necessarily mean lack of talent!) How would they deal with youngsters who did not want their classmates to know about their area of talent? (Listening is important here...some pupils will welcome being coaxed to perform, while others really wish to be left alone.)

Great ideas and useful strategies for identifying, developing and supporting talented pupils

In a recent workshop one of the teachers shared her school's idea of involving pupils in teaching their teachers to play 'their' musical instrument. This raised teachers' awareness of how difficult it is to play well (and to remember to practise!), and led to a joint concert (staff and their 'tutors') at the end of the year.

Make a note of other useful strategies... (One of the best things about INSET days, conferences and workshops is the opportunity to share good ideas with colleagues!)

©2005 Bette Gray-Fow

Talent Audit

Inclusivity versus elitism

Practical issues
TIME

TRAINING

EQUIPMENT/RESOURCES

Meeting the individual needs of talented pupils:

Great ideas and useful strategies for identifying, developing and supporting talented pupils

©2005 Bette Gray-Fow

National Curriculum guidelines for identifying talented pupils in PE, music, and art and design

The National Curriculum online website contains a wealth of useful information to do with gifted and talented pupils in PE, music and art and design, including ideas for challenging able pupils in these subjects, and the following lists of characteristics.

(This Appendix is taken from QCA guidelines and is reproduced by kind permission of QCA Enterprises.)

Identifying gifted and talented learners: general guidance

What does 'gifted and talented' mean?

There are many definitions of gifted and talented. This guidance builds on the work of *Excellence in Cities* (*EiC*), which identifies:

- 'gifted' learners as those who have abilities in one or more subjects in the statutory school curriculum other than art and design, music and PE;
- 'talented' learners as those who have abilities in art and design, music, PE, or performing arts such as dance and drama.

This guidance uses the phrase 'gifted and talented' to describe all learners with gifts and talents.

EiC targets gifted and talented work at the top five to ten per cent of pupils in any school, regardless of the overall ability profile of pupils. Many schools and local education authorities outside *EiC* have adopted similar criteria, while others use alternative benchmarks.

While the *EiC* definition relates to the National Curriculum and to pupils of compulsory school age, it may be extended to include those who show marked abilities in any area of the school or college curriculum at any age. It is not unusual for older students to show significant ability and enthusiasm when they take up new areas of the curriculum and have a new context for study.

The *Excellence Challenge* (now known as the Aimhigher Programme) takes a similar approach to *Excellence in Cities* in respect of gifted and talented 16- to 19-year-olds, but targets the top 2 to 20 per cent of students in an institution.

Identifying pupils talented in PE

Pupils who are talented in PE are likely to show many or all of the following characteristics in their performance and approach to PE, sport and dance.

Approach to work

They may:

- be confident in themselves and in familiar contexts;
- take risks with ideas and approaches, and be able to think 'outside the box';
- show a high degree of motivation and commitment to practice and performance.

Effective performance

They may:

- be intelligent, independent, thoughtful performers, actively forming and adapting strategies, tactics or compositions;
- be able to reflect on processes and outcomes in order to improve performance, understanding the close and changing relationship between skill, fitness and the tactics or composition of their performance;
- be creative, original and adaptable, responding quickly to new challenges and situations, and often finding new and innovative solutions to them.

Body skilfulness and awareness

They may:

- have a high degree of control and co-ordination of their bodies;
- show strong awareness of their body in space;
- combine movements fluently, precisely and accurately in a range of contexts and activities.

Some pupils may have unusual abilities in specific aspects of the programme of study or areas of activity, such as:

- evaluating and improving performance through leadership;
- acquiring, developing and performing advanced skills and techniques;
- conceptual understanding, shown through the sophisticated selection and application of advanced skills, tactics and compositional ideas for their age;

- particularly high levels of fitness for their age, in both specific and general areas;
- specific strengths in general areas, such as games activities or dance activities.

Some pupils perform at high levels in sport or dance in the community, for example basketball, high jump, jazz dance or sailing. In some cases, these pupils' performance may be too specific to be easily related to the National Curriculum level descriptions for PE.

Teachers should be aware that age and physical maturation can lead to better performance at certain ages and stages, but they are not a characteristic of talent in PE and sport.

Identifying pupils talented in music

Pupils who are talented in music are likely to:

- be captivated by sound and engage fully with music;
- select an instrument with care and then be unwilling to relinquish the instrument;
- find it difficult not to respond physically to music;
- memorise music quickly without any apparent effort, be able to repeat more complex rhythmical and melodic phrases given by the teacher and repeat melodies (sometimes after one hearing);
- sing and play music with a natural awareness of the musical phrase – the music makes sense;
- demonstrate the ability to communicate through music, for example to sing with musical expression and with confidence;
- show strong preferences, single-mindedness and a sustained inner drive to make music.

Pupils more often show their musical talent through the quality of their response than the complexity of their response. Musical quality is very difficult to define in words, as music is a different form of communication to language. The closest we can get is to say that it 'sounds right': skills and techniques are used to communicate an intended mood or effect.

Therefore musical talent is at least as much about demonstrating a higher quality response *within* levels as about attainment at higher levels. Musical talent can be seen at every level of attainment.

Pupils who have a talent for music show a particular affinity with sound. This type of talent is sometimes hard to identify, especially when it is not combined with more general giftedness. It is, however, often most significant, since it may be a pupil's only route to real success, increasing their self-esteem and motivation for other areas of learning.

Some research points to the fact that there may be different types of intelligence, and that each of us may be more intelligent in some areas than others. This is often the case in music – talented musicians may not demonstrate talent or giftedness in other areas.

Some teachers believe that music is only accessible for pupils with talent: that pupils are either musical, or not musical. This is not the case. All pupils can develop musical skills, knowledge and understanding. Some may need more or less help, but this is no different from any other subject. Teachers need to recognise the different needs of all pupils, including not only those who are talented but those who are more generally gifted across several subjects. The musically talented will need appropriate extension and development, while the more generally gifted pupils will need challenging musical contexts that enable them to apply their more general abilities.

Music provides a context in which generically gifted pupils (that is, those who are more generally gifted across several subjects) can be identified and developed. In music, pupils have to deal with a complex range of different and simultaneous factors and bring them together when making and responding to music, using skills which are often associated with giftedness. Teachers have often commented on the way that quickness in remembering rhythmic patterns suggests the ability to think quickly and assimilate information. Similarly, a difficulty with remembering patterns can indicate learning difficulties across all subjects – teachers have found that music can help them to identify children who may need help.

Because music is abstract, it provides a way of identifying and developing skills that are not language dependent. This means that it can play a particularly important part in helping to recognise giftedness in pupils whose language skills have not yet developed, especially those for whom English is not their first language.

Recognising talent in music

Musical talent may not be a constant potential that can be realised at any age. If the talent is to be fulfilled, it may have to be recognised at an early stage. This is especially true for some instrumental skills that require early development.

In secondary schools, there may be talented pupils who have not been recognised. These pupils need to be identified as early as possible, to ensure that their abilities are developed. In many cases, this will include providing opportunities for instrumental tuition for those who show musical talent.

Pupils who have already been having specialist lessons may present further challenges and will need to be encouraged to bring their instrumental skills into the classroom. Often the hardest challenge is to help these pupils balance their high levels of skill in performing on an instrument with the development of broader musical skills, knowledge and understanding, for example through creative activities.

Identifying pupils talented in art and design

Pupils who are talented in art and design are likely to:

- **think and express themselves in creative, original ways** – they want to follow a different plan to the other pupils, challenge the tasks given, or extend the brief in seemingly unrelated or fantastic directions;

- **have a strong desire to create in a visual form** – they are driven by ideas, imagination, flights of fancy, humanitarian concerns, humour or personal experience; they persevere until they have completed a task successfully, with little or no intervention from the teacher;

- **push the boundaries of normal processes** – they test ideas and solve problems relating to concepts and issues; they explore ways to depict ideas, emotions, feelings and meanings; they take risks without knowing what the outcome will be; they change ideas to take into account new influences or outcomes;

- **show a passionate interest in the world of art and design** – they are often interested in a specific culture (possibly relating to their own cultural background or sense of identity), particular art forms, contemporary culture or youth culture;

- **use materials, tools and techniques skilfully and learn new approaches easily** – they are keen to extend their technical abilities and sometimes get frustrated when other skills do not develop at the same time;

- **initiate ideas and define problems** – they explore ideas, problems and sources on their own and collaboratively, with a sense of purpose and meaning;

- **critically evaluate visual work and other information** – they make unusual connections between their own and others' work; they apply ideas to their own work in innovative ways;

- **exploit the characteristics of materials and processes** – they use materials and processes in creative, practical and inventive ways; they explore alternatives and respond to new possibilities and meanings;

- **understand that ideas and meanings in their own and others' work can be interpreted in different ways** – they use their knowledge and understanding to extend their own thinking and realise their intentions; they communicate original ideas, insights and views.

The Sheffield Project
Identifying musically talented primary school pupils

The materials that follow are exact replicas of some of those used in the Sheffield Project discussed in Chapter 7. Following the project outline (below), there is a list of **Instructions for Administering the Music Listening Quiz**, a **Self-evaluation Form** and a **Request for Instrumental Lessons**. In addition to these materials, participating teachers also received a 20-minute CD of music for the Music Listening Quiz, a test paper to photocopy, and marking guidelines.

Project outline: the overall strategy

1. To raise pupil awareness of music through a series of activities, some 'high profile', some very low-key.
2. To allow sufficient time between activities/events, so that pupils are not swayed by the enthusiasm of the moment.
3. To positively encourage boys to participate in instrumental lessons, e.g. by applying selection criteria flexibly, to make sure that boys do not feel isolated.
4. To address a number of issues to do with retention in the instrumental tuition programme, e.g. by raising parental/pupil awareness of what is involved, offering funding opportunities for continuing with lessons, trying to match the instruments offered with the overall needs of the school's music programme, etc.
5. To encourage links to aid in transition to destination secondary schools, e.g. through visits by secondary school musicians to their feeder primary schools.

Phase one

Workshop with visiting artists – staff to observe pupils informally for rhythmic co-ordination, engagement (particularly attentiveness/enthusiasm). Really a 'taster' for what it is like to perform, and a screening mechanism for those whose co-ordination and/or attentiveness might prove to be an obstacle to success in instrumental lessons.

Phase two

Classroom exercise in responding to a **Music Listening Quiz**, featuring a wide variety of music. Teachers to observe (and comment on, if appropriate) engagement/interest during the exercise.

Materials

- CD of music for the Listening Quiz
- Instructions for Administering the Test
- Photocopies of the test paper (one for each pupil)

Phase three

Visits to target primary schools (either in whole-school assembly or to particular classes, depending on logistics/availability) of related secondary school music teacher and pupil musician(s), so children can see older pupils playing an instrument and talking about why they enjoy learning to play. (Role modelling with older pupils.)

Phase four

Towards the end of the Summer Term, let class know that there may be an opportunity to have instrumental lessons in the autumn. Probably best presented in class, and not in assembly – again, in a low-key way, to avoid putting excessive peer pressure on pupils (especially boys).

Interested pupils to see the teacher for a **Self-evaluation Form** and **Request for Instrumental Lessons** to take home to discuss and sign. Make it clear that we do not know exactly what instruments will be available for that school, but provide a list of likely possibilities. (Not saxophone!) Collect at lunch hour, break, or after school so that children have to make an effort to attend.

Return signed forms to [......................................], together with any other information regarding the pupils (i.e. those that have been positively identified from the workshop and listening exercise).

Materials

- Self-evaluation Form
- Request for Instrumental Lessons

Phase five

Evaluate forms using the marking guidelines. Then discuss with Music Service what instrumental provision is available/possible for individual schools.

Phase six

Let pupils know what instruments are available for their school, and if possible allow some choice within that. Some pupils may not be interested at that point; in which case we could look to those who were lower in the ranking.

Instructions for Administering the Music Listening Quiz

Pupils will need the following materials:

- pencil and rubber
- coloured pens/pencils (optional – if choosing the drawing option on the last question)
- a copy of the test paper.

Administering the quiz

The CD contains 20 minutes of music. To include time to read the questions, to repeat tracks if necessary, and for the final question, you should allow 35 minutes to administer the quiz.

This quiz is designed to be used with a variety of literacy levels. Questions relate to individual tracks on the CD. This means you can repeat a CD track if you feel pupils need more time to write. You might want to read out the introductions (and even the multiple choice answers) and discuss them with pupils, if you feel it would help their understanding.

Aims

This is not a 'test' with 'right' or 'wrong' answers! No one can 'fail'. In fact, one aim is to make children feel that they are 'good at music'. Another aim is for pupils to listen to a wide range of music, and to feel they've learned something from the experience.

It is important to present the quiz as an *experiment* – that the papers will be sent off to a university, because we're curious about their responses. They must not feel pressured by feeling they are being 'selected'.

One section has some complex questions designed to discriminate between pupils who can hear detailed musical textures, and those who find this more difficult. But hopefully this will not put anyone off.

We are looking for *quality of response to the music*, and for engagement with the task. Most pupils this age should engage well with the task; but it would be helpful if you would note on the pupil's script if they were particularly inattentive, or found the quiz boring or frustrating to complete. The extracts are all about two minutes long, to see whether pupils' attention wanders, or whether they become engrossed in the music.

Completed papers and the CD should be returned to [..], who will forward them on to me.

Remember – the aim is not to 'select' just a few youngsters, but to spread the net rather wider. Hopefully at the end of the various elements of the programme, we will have a long list of pupils who might benefit from extra music tuition, or for musical opportunities in secondary school.

Again, many thanks for your continued help with this project.

Bette Gray-Fow, Creative Arts Team Leader, The Open University

---

Please feed back any comments you may have, e.g. on language level, length, content, clarity of instructions, pupils' response, etc. The quiz is very much in the developmental stage, and we value very highly your thoughts and observations.

Self-evaluation Form

Name _____ Class _____

Learning to play or sing

Learning to play or sing really well needs more than a good voice or making a good sound on an instrument.

It takes a lot of hard work, time and patience! In fact, some people who don't make the best sounds at first, turn out to be the best players and singers in the end.

Do **you** have what it takes?

Test yourself!

	Usually	Sometimes	Not often
I follow directions well.			
I remember to bring my work to school.			
I work well in small groups.			
I think I can find some time at home or in break times to practice.			
I like to listen to music.			

Request for Instrumental Lessons

It is also important for people at home to know about what is needed to learn to play an instrument well. For a start, it does not sound too great at first! It takes TIME to master an instrument. And you need to feel comfortable about making mistakes at first.

So people listening to practice must not be too impatient. When the going gets a bit tough, you need lots of support and encouragement from the folks at home.

Talk over these issues at home. If your parents/carers feel able to support you in learning an instrument, ask them to sign below, and return the form to your class teacher. We will then speak to the Music Service, to see how many instrumental places will be available this year. If you do not get a chance to learn this time around, your name will be passed on to your secondary school, for another chance there.

I would like my son/daughter, ..., to be considered for instrumental music lessons at school. I will do my best to make sure they have the time to practice, and that they look after the instrument while it is on loan.

Parent/Carer _____ Date _____

I would like to learn an instrument at school. I will do my best to attend regularly and to practise my skills in between lessons.

Pupil _____

Guidance on writing whole-school and departmental policies for talent identification and development

Whole-school and departmental policies can serve a number of purposes:

- the process of considering issues and agreeing on policies and procedures gives staff the opportunity to think in some depth about a range of theoretical and practical concerns;
- once written, the policy can be a useful point of reference, e.g. it may set out conditions under which extra support might be given, or clarify the range of strategies to be used across departments and/or across the whole school;
- a well-written policy can be a good way of communicating both the school's goals and its procedures (e.g. for selecting pupils for the school's register of gifted and talented pupils) to parents, to pupils and to the wider community;
- clarifying underlying principles means that when new issues arise there is some common ground for discussion.

A separate whole-school policy for the talent realm?

Many schools have reported that they have found the talent areas to be problematic, in terms of both identification and provision. This is partly owing to the distinctive nature of the talent area.

Conventional testing procedures are reasonably effective in identifying pupils with the capacity for academic success. When used in conjunction with a range of other methods (e.g. teacher recommendation) and with respect for issues such as the pupil's use of English as a second language, and special needs such as dyslexia, we can be fairly certain that a large proportion of able pupils will be 'identifiable' by some means or another.

Yet for the talent areas – and also for 'creativity' – tests are not so well developed or reliable. The most effective strategy for identifying talent is first to expose the pupils to sustained training, and then to see how their talents develop over a period of time.

Policies for identifying and nurturing pupils' talents are often included in whole-school 'able pupil' policies. Yet there are real differences between the ways in which ability develops in the creative arts and sport, as opposed to more academic pursuits. For example, it is the business of *all* primary schools to train pupils in academic skills, such as literacy, numeracy and so on; yet the lack of specialist teaching in the arts and sport means that in many schools children will not be receiving sustained access to high-level coaching in these areas. Although this situation is changing gradually (e.g. as government initiatives to widen opportunities in the arts and sport become more widespread), for many pupils, high-quality provision for all of the talent areas will continue to be in short supply. Unless there is a strong interest in a talent area in the child's home, his or her talent is unlikely to show.

In my own view there is a case to be made for having a separate **whole-school policy** (or a section of a whole-school policy) **dedicated to talent identification and development**. This would address the needs of all pupils, not just those showing high ability in the creative arts or sport; improve awareness of the benefits to be gained from participation in these areas; and reinforce the whole school's commitment to developing pupils' talents.

Within **subject departments**, policies for talent identification and development will normally be part of a more specialised 'able pupil policy'. This means that a more detailed set of guidelines and principles can be agreed, tailored to the needs of specific curriculum areas, and dealing with issues such as extracurricular provision, links with outside bodies and so on. These might incorporate the National Curriculum guidelines for identifying talented pupils (see Appendix B) and address strategies for identifying and tracking pupils in the particular area, e.g. through an 'able pupil checklist' for art, sport or music, or by using self-reporting (see pp. 110–12).

Materials for use in whole-school and departmental policies for talented pupils

In practice, many schools formulate their policies by looking at examples used in other schools, adapting them for their own context. Here are some materials for use as a resource in constructing or adapting school and departmental policies to take account of some of the special characteristics and needs of the talent area.

A sample whole-school policy on talent identification and development

- We as a school recognise the many benefits of pupils' participation in sport and the creative arts.
- The talent areas provide a range of benefits for pupils who take part: self-expression, confidence, dedication, teamwork, good health and fitness, enjoyment.
- Talent development involves a serious commitment to regular training and practice. We as a school will endeavour to support pupils with these commitments, by offering (where possible) curriculum flexibility to develop individual strengths.

- Since exceptional talent will not show itself without developing the necessary skills over time, we will endeavour to provide all pupils with a range of opportunities to experience the creative arts and sport at first hand. Where possible this will be on a sustained basis, and open to all who wish to participate.
- As a school we value the achievements of our talented pupils, and endeavour to recognise and celebrate their successes, whether achieved within school or in the wider community.

A sample departmental policy on/for talent identification and development

Rationale:

- We recognise that exceptional artistic/musical/sporting achievement is a combination of natural ability, training and a commitment to sustained practice; and that the full extent of a pupil's talents will only show with sustained input of time, training and effort.
- We also recognise the many benefits of participation in art/music/sport for every pupil, not just for those of exceptional ability or those who have had prior training.
- We therefore aim to provide opportunities both within the curriculum and in extracurricular activities for all of our pupils to develop their artistic/musical/sporting talents, and to develop and reinforce the task commitment necessary to make the most of these talents.

Our procedures for identifying talented pupils include:

(a) Transition information from primary schools.

(b) Systematic collection and recording of information on talent development which pupils are involved in outside school, e.g. local sports clubs, piano lessons, choir at a local church, summer schools in a range of artistic pursuits, etc.

(c) An awareness that testing procedures in the talent areas can be flawed, and should not be relied on excessively.

(d) Teacher, parent and peer recommendations.

(e) Recognising those pupils showing serious commitment to an area of talent, as well as those showing particular flair and ability.

(f) Taking account of the particular needs of late developers, i.e. not to focus solely on those with precocious development.

Provision for talent development in the department includes:

(a) Within the curriculum, a range of differentiated materials and approaches to stretch the able, and to extend and enrich their role within practical activities in the classroom.

(b) Outside the curriculum, a range of extracurricular activities to enhance and extend the curriculum [insert here a list of activities appropriate to your subject department].

(c) A clear policy on participation and progression, including groups or activities which are open to all, and those which require an audition, trial or recommendation.

(d) Clear guidelines for promoting task commitment and avoiding the 'prima donna effect', including, for example:

   – pupils who are members of teams will not be allowed to play unless they have attended training that week (or x number of rehearsals that term);

   – students who use the art room are responsible for clearing up afterwards; pupils with a leading role in a school production have an obligation to attend rehearsals and to learn their lines, as specified in the rehearsal schedule;

   – members of the (select) Chamber Singers are expected to continue their participation in School Choir.

   Note: an exception to this might be made for pupils who are totally overwhelmed with performing commitments inside or outside school; or whose instrumental/vocal teachers are reluctant to allow them to participate in ensembles at a particular stage of their development. In this case it can be helpful to negotiate another visible role for them in the department, so they are seen to contribute to the programme as a whole; for example, by occasionally helping out with sectional rehearsals, or helping to supervise younger pupils backstage at a concert. The same applies to young sports men and women who are prohibited by their clubs from participating in school teams.

(e) A commitment to supporting pupils' artistic/musical/sporting development by providing the highest quality training for talented pupils, whether within the curriculum, in extracurricular groups, or, where appropriate, through referral to outside specialists and agencies.

References and further reading

Abbott, A. and Collins, D. (2002) 'A theoretical and empirical analysis of a "state of the art" talent identification model', *High Ability Studies* 13(2), 157–78.

Balyi, I. (2003) 'Long-term athlete development: the system and solutions', *FHS* 14: www.youthsporttrust.org/talentladder/ talentladder_2003/IstvanBalyi_LTAD.pdf

Beckham, D. with Watt, T. (2003) *David Beckham: My Side*. London: CollinsWillow (an imprint of HarperCollins).

Bee, P. (2003) 'Even winners can be losers: athletes risk being plagued by a wide range of health complaints after retirement', T2 supplement in *The Times*, 22 October.

Bragg, M. *et al.* (1993) *The Great Dance Collection: Sylvie Guillem* (Video). Edited and presented by Melvyn Bragg; produced and directed by Nigel Watts; background notes by Margaret Willis (1995). Produced by LWTP with RM Arts. Manufactured, sold and distributed in the UK by Polygram Record Operations Ltd.

Campbell, D. (1997) *The Mozart Effect*. New York: Avon Books.

Carter, J. E. L. and Ackland, T. T. (eds) (1994) *Kinanthropometry in Aquatic Sports: A Study of World Class Athletes*. Champaign, IL: Human Kinetics.

Catterall, J. S., Chapleau, R. and Iwanaga, J. (1999) 'Involvement in the arts and human development: general involvement and intensive involvement in music and theater arts', in E. B. Fiske (ed.) *Champions of Change: The Impact of the Arts on Learning*. Washington, DC: The Arts Education Partnership, The President's Committee on the Arts and the Humanities, pp. 1–18.

Clark, C. and Callow, R. (2002) *Educating the Gifted and Talented* (2nd edn). London: David Fulton Publishers.

Clark, G. and Zimmerman, E. (1994) 'What do we know about artistically talented students and their teachers?', *Journal of Art & Design Education* 13(3), 275–86.

Colangelo, N. and Davis, G. (eds) (2003) *Handbook of Gifted Education* (3rd edn). Boston, MA: Allyn & Bacon.

Couger, J. (1996) *Creativity and Innovation*. Boston, MA: Boyd & Fraser.

Davidson, J. W., Howe, M. J. A. and Moore, D. G. (1996) 'The role of parental influences in the development of musical ability', *British Journal of Developmental Psychology* 14, 399–412.

DES (Department of Education and Science) (1967) *Children and their Primary*

Schools: A Report of the Central Advisory Council for Education (England). London: HMSO.

Ericsson, K. A. (1996) 'The acquisition of expert performance: an introduction to some of the issues', in K. A. Ericsson (ed.) *The Road to Excellence: The Acquisition of Expert Performance in the Arts and Sciences, Sports and Games.* Mahwah, NJ: Lawrence Erlbaum, pp. 1–50.

Eyre, D. (1997) *Able Children in Ordinary Schools.* London: NACE/David Fulton Publishers.

Eyre, D. and Lowe, H. (eds) (2002) *Curriculum Provision for the Gifted and Talented in the Secondary School.* London: NACE/David Fulton Publishers.

Freeman, J. (2001) *Gifted Children Grown Up.* London: David Fulton Publishers.

Gagné, F. (1991) 'Toward a differentiated model of giftedness and talent', in N. Colangelo and G. A. Davis (eds) *Handbook of Gifted Education.* Boston, MA: Allyn and Bacon, pp. 65–80.

Gagné, F. (1993) 'Constructs and models pertaining to exceptional human abilities', in K. A. Heller *et al.* (eds) *International Handbook of Giftedness and Talent.* Oxford: Pergamon Press, pp. 63–85.

Gagné, F. (1999) 'Nature or nurture? A re-examination of Sloboda and Howe's (1991) interview study on talent development in music', *Psychology of Music* 27(1), 38–51.

Gagné, F. (2000) 'Understanding the complex choreography of talent development through DMGT-based analysis', in K. A. Heller *et al.* (eds) *International Handbook of Giftedness and Talent* (2nd edn). Oxford: Elsevier Science Ltd, pp. 67–79.

Gardner, H. (1983) *Frames of Mind: The Theory of Multiple Intelligences.* New York: Basic Books.

Gardner, H. (1993a) *Frames of Mind* (2nd edition). London: Fontana Press.

Gardner, H. (1993b) *Multiple Intelligences: The Theory in Practice.* New York: Basic Books.

Gardner, H. (1997) *Extraordinary Minds.* London: Phoenix.

Gardner, H. (1999) *Intelligence Reframed: Multiple Intelligences for the 21st Century.* New York: Basic Books.

George, D. (1997) *The Challenge of the Able Child* (2nd edn). London: David Fulton Publishers.

Goleman, D. (1995) *Emotional Intelligence: Why It Can Matter More Than IQ.* New York: Bantam.

Gray, K. M. and Kunkel, M. A. (2001) 'The experience of female ballet dancers: a grounded theory', *High Ability Studies* 12(1), 7–25.

Harland, J., Kinder, K., Lord, P., Stott, A., Schagen, I., Haynes, J., Cusworth, L., White, R. and Paola, R. (2000) 'Research summary', in *Arts Education in Secondary Schools: Effects and Effectiveness.* Slough: NFER, pp. 1–14.

Haroutounian, J. (2000a) 'Perspectives of musical talent: a study of identification criteria and procedures', *High Ability Studies* 11(2), 137–60.

Haroutounian, J. (2000b) 'The delights and dilemmas of the musically talented teenager', *Journal of Secondary Gifted Education* 12(1), 3–17.

Heller, K. A. *et al.* (eds) *International Handbook of Giftedness and Talent* (2nd edn). Oxford: Elsevier Science Ltd.

Howe, M. J. A., Davidson, J. W. and Sloboda, J. A. (1998) 'Innate talents: reality or myth?', *Behavioural and Brain Sciences* **21**(3), 399–407.

Hymer, B. with Michel, D. (2002) *Gifted and Talented Learners: Creating a Policy for Inclusion*. London: David Fulton Publishers.

Institute of Youth Sport (2001a) *Physical Education, Cognitive Development and Academic Performance*. Leeds: Human Kinetics.

Institute of Youth Sport (2001b) *Parental Influence in Physical Activity and Sport*. Loughborough: Institute of Youth Sport.

Institute of Youth Sport (2001c) *Talent Identification, Selection and Development*. Loughborough: Institute of Youth Sport.

Karpf, A. (2002) 'Gift Rapped', G2 supplement in *Guardian*, 6 March, p. 7.

Kohn, A. (1999) *Punished by Rewards: The Trouble with Gold Stars, Incentive Plans, A's, Praise and Other Bribes*. New York: Houghton Mifflin.

Lamont, A. *et al.* (2001) *Young People and Music Participation*. Report funded by the Economic and Social Research Council. Keele: Unit for the Study of Musical Skill and Development, Keele University.

Leyden, S. (1998) *Supporting the Child of Exceptional Ability*. London: David Fulton Publishers.

McEnroe, J. with Kaplan, J. (2003) *Serious: The Autobiography*. London: Time Warner Books UK.

Maree, J. G. and Ebersohn, L. (2002) 'Emotional intelligence and achievement: redefining giftedness', *Gifted Education International* **16**(3).

Montgomery, D. (ed.) (2000) *Able Underachievers*. London: Whurr Publishers.

Morgan, W. P. (1980) 'Test of champions: the iceberg profile', *Psychology Today* **14**, 92–108.

Morley, S. (2001) *The Authorised Biography of John Gielgud*. London: Hodder & Stoughton.

Morrison, A. and Johnston, B. (2003) 'Personal creativity for entrepreneurship: teaching and learning strategies', *Active Learning in Higher Education* **4**(2), 145–58.

Murphy, C. (2002) 'How far do tests of musical ability shed light on the nature of musical intelligence?', in G. Spruce (ed.) *Aspects of Teaching Secondary Music: Perspectives on Practice*. London: Routledge Falmer/The Open University, pp. 66–78.

NACCCE (National Advisory Committee of Creative Cultural Education) (1999) *All our Futures: Creativity, Culture and Education*. Report to the Secretary of State for Education and Employment and the Secretary of State for Culture, Media and Sport. London: HMSO.

NATA (National Athletic Trainers' Association) (1995) *Press Release: Researchers Assess Risk of Suicide Among Injured Student Athletes* (25 January): www.nata.org/publications/press_releases/researcher_suicide_study.htm (accessed April 2004). For full text of article, see *Journal of Athletic Training*, 30(1) (January–March 1995).

Nieuwenhuis, C. F., Spamer, E. J. and Van Rossum, J. H. A. (2002) 'Prediction function for identifying talent in 14- to 15-year-old female field hockey players', *High Ability Studies* **13**(1), 21–33.

Noice, T. and Noice, H. (2002) 'The expertise of professional actors: a review of recent research', *High Ability Studies* **13**(1), 7–19.

Nuttall, N. (1998) 'Musicians develop more brainpower', *The Times*, 23 April.

O'Brien, P. (2003) *Using Science to Develop Thinking Skills at Key Stage 3*. London: David Fulton Publishers.

Odam, G. (1995) *The Sounding Symbol*. London: Stanley Thornes (Publishers) Ltd.

Ofsted (2001a) *Providing for Gifted and Talented Pupils: An Evaluation of Excellence in Cities and Other Grant-funded Programmes*, HMI 334. London: Ofsted.

Ofsted (2001b) *Specialist Schools: An Evaluation of Progress*. London: Ofsted.

Ofsted (2003) *Excellence in Cities and Education Action Zones: Management and Impact*, HMI 1399. London: Ofsted.

Ofsted and Youth Support Trust (2000) *Sports Colleges: The First Two Years*. London: HMSO.

Ostwald, P. F. (1998) *Glenn Gould: The Ecstasy and Tragedy of Genius*. New York: W. W. Norton.

Pomerantz, M. and Pomerantz, K. (2002) *Listening to Underachievers*. London: David Fulton Publishers.

QCA (Qualifications and Curriculum Authority) (2001) *Press Release: PE and Sport Project* (27 March)
www.qca.org.uk/news/2586_1720.html (accessed April 2004).

Rauscher, F., Shaw, G., Levine, L., Write, E., Dennis, W. and Newcomb, R. (1997) 'Music training causes long-term enhancement of preschool children's spatial-temporal reasoning', *Neurological Research* **19**, 2–8.

Redfield Jamison, K. (1996) *Touched with Fire: Manic Depressive Illness and the Artistic Temperament* (Reissue edition). New York: Free Press.

Robson, A. (2003) Letter, *ISM Music Journal* **70**(3), 105.

Rosenthal, R. and Jacobson, L. (1968) *Pygmalion in the Classroom: Teacher Expectation and Pupils' Intellectual Development*. New York: Rinehart and Winston. (Expanded edition published in 1992 by Irvington Publishers, New York.)

Rostan, S., Pariser, D. and Gruber, H. E. (2002) 'A cross-cultural study of the development of artistic talent, creativity and giftedness', *High Ability Studies* **13**(2), 125–55.

Seeley, K. (1996) 'The arts and talent development', *Gifted Education International* **11**(3), 136–8.

Shuter-Dyson, R. and Gabriel, C. (1981) *The Psychology of Musical Ability*. London: Methuen.

Sloboda, J. A. (1985) *The Musical Mind*. Oxford: Oxford University Press.

Sloboda, J. A. (1996) 'The acquisition of musical performance expertise: deconstructing the "talent" account of individual differences in musical expressivity', in K. A. Ericsson (ed.) *The Road to Excellence: The Acquisition of*

Expert Performance in the Arts and Sciences, Sports and Games. Mahwah, NJ: Lawrence Erlbaum, pp. 107–26.

Sloboda, J. A. and Howe, J. A. (1992) 'Transition in the early musical careers of able young musicians: choosing instrument and teachers', *Journal of Research in Music Education* 40(4), 283–94.

SportScotland (2002) *Talent Identification and Development: An Academic Review*. Edinburgh: SportScotland (for a summary of content see www.sportscotland.org.uk/pdfdocuments/talentidentificationanddevelop_summary.pdf).

Sternberg, R. (1997) *Thinking Styles*. Cambridge: Cambridge University Press.

Sternberg, R. J. (ed.) (1999) *Handbook of Creativity*. Cambridge: Cambridge University Press.

Sternberg, R. J. (2001) 'Giftedness as developing expertise: theory of the interface between high abilities and achieved excellence', *High Ability Studies* 12(2), 159–79.

Sternberg, R. J. and Lubart, T. I. (1999) 'The concept of creativity: prospects and paradigms', in R. J. Sternberg (ed.) *Handbook of Creativity*. Cambridge: Cambridge University Press, pp. 3–15.

Stopper, M. J. (ed.) (2000) *Meeting the Social and Emotional Needs of Gifted and Talented Children*. London: David Fulton Publishers.

Tannenbaum, A. J. (1983) *Gifted Children: Psychological and Educational Perspectives*. New York: Macmillan.

Technology Colleges Trust (2000) *Best Practice in Technology Colleges: A Guide to School Improvement*. London: Technology Colleges Trust.

Technology Colleges Trust (2002) *Best Practice in Arts Colleges: A Guide to School Improvement*. London: Technology Colleges Trust (reprinted with amendments by Specialist Schools Trust, 2003).

Unit for the Study of Musical Skill and Development (2001) *Young People and Music Participation Report*. Keele: Keele University.

Van Rossum, J. H. A. (2001) 'Talented in dance: the Bloom Stage Model revisited in the personal histories of dance students', *High Ability Studies* 12(2), 181–97.

Van Tassel-Baska, J. (2001) 'The talent development process: what we know and what we don't know', *Gifted Education International* 16(1), 20–8.

Wallace, B. (ed.) (2003) *Using History to Develop Thinking Skills at Key Stage 2*. London: David Fulton Publishers.

Winner, E. and Martino, G. (2000) 'Giftedness in non-academic domains: the case of the visual arts and music', in K. A. Heller *et al.* (eds) *International Handbook of Giftedness and Talent* (2nd edn). Oxford: Elsevier Science Ltd, pp. 95–110.

Winner, E. and Martino, G. (2003) 'Artistic giftedness', in N. Colangelo and G. A. Davis (eds) *Handbook of Gifted Education* (3rd edn). Boston, MA: Allyn & Bacon, pp. 335–49.

Woody, R. (2004) 'The motivations of exceptional musicians', *MENC* (The National Association for Music Education Journal), 1 February: www.menc.org/publication/articles/journals.html

Ziegler, A. and Raul, T. (2000) 'Myth and reality: a review of empirical studies on giftedness', *High Ability Studies* 11(2), 113–36.

Index